Market Participant Perspectives

Selections from Mercer Capital's
Financial Reporting Blog

Market Participant Perspectives

Selections from Mercer Capital's
Financial Reporting Blog

ISBN: 978-0-9825364-5-2

Peabody Publishing LP
5100 Poplar Avenue
Suite 2600
Memphis, Tennessee 38137
901.685.2120

Table of Contents

SECTION III: PURCHASE PRICE ALLOCATIONS & INTANGIBLES

SECTION IV: PORTFOLIO VALUATION

Table of Contents

Introduction

We started writing weekly about fair value reporting in 2013 on our *Financial Reporting Blog*. We are a valuation firm with an active and growing practice helping our public and private company clients prepare fair value measurements for financial reporting. While not knowing exactly what we were getting into, we hoped that the discipline of weekly commentary on topics related to fair value measurement would keep us sharp and prove helpful for our clients and friends. Looking back over more than three years and 150 posts, it seemed an opportune time to review our posts and compile what might, for lack of a better term, be called a "Greatest Hits" collection of our favorites.

The posts in this collection are grouped by primary topic:

- **Fair Value & Regulatory**. Fair value measurement stands at the intersection of economic analysis and regulatory compliance. Between the FASB, IASB, SEC and PCAOB, there has been no shortage of new developments to summarize and analyze.

- **Impairment Testing**. In M&A, as in life, things don't always work out the way one had hoped. The shift from amortization to an impairment model for goodwill in the early 2000s made fair value measurement of reporting units a critical topic for CFOs and auditors.

- **Purchase Price Allocation and Intangibles**. Adopting the purchase method of accounting put the spotlight on valuing identifiable intangible assets. From customer relationships to tradenames to intellectual property to contingent consideration, purchase price allocation assignments generate some of the most interesting questions we and our clients face.

- **Portfolio Valuation**. Private equity, hedge, and venture capital funds report the fair value of portfolio holdings to investors and regulators on a periodic basis. The continual re-measurement of fair value marks from purchase through sale creates unique challenges for fund managers.

- **Equity Compensation**. Translating pay packages denominated in shares and other equity instruments into dollar-denominated compensation expense has consequences for both reporting companies and their employees.

We have selected the posts in this collection with an eye toward mirroring the breadth of our service offerings. This book is not, however, intended as a comprehensive technical guide for fair value measurement. Blog posts are, by their nature, occasional: some analyze current transactions from a fair value perspective, while others are more general reflections prompted by recurring themes in our engagements. We have no pretensions of being the next John LeCarre, but a quick glance at the Table of Contents should reveal that we aim for a tone that is lively rather than pedantic.

For our existing clients and blog subscribers, we hope that this book uncovers a post or two of interest that you might have missed the first time around. For clients that we haven't met yet, there's probably no better introduction to our team than the collection of posts in this book. As you will see from the breadth of contributors to this effort, we have assembled a great group of thoughtful, hardworking professionals focused on serving our clients. Let us know how we can help you.

Travis W. Harms, CFA, CPA/ABV
901.685.2120 | harmst@mercercapital.com

Fair Value & Regulatory

Non-GAAP Measures: Here to Stay?

Lucas Parris, CFA, ASA-BV/IA
Originally Published on May 23, 2016

The debate over the use of non-GAAP performance measures continues. Even as the prevalence of these items grows in the financial reports of public companies (and those that want to be), cautionary tales of the uses and abuses of such metrics garner headlines. A recent *New York Times* piece entitled "Fantasy Math Is Helping Companies Spin Losses Into Profits" pretty much sums up one side of the issue with its headline alone. [1]

The NYT piece focuses on companies that provided measures of "adjusted earnings" which had been adjusted to remove items like stock-based compensation expense, restructuring costs, asset write-downs, and other items that the subject company considers unusual or non-recurring. Citing a study performed by The Analyst's Accounting Observer, 30 companies on the S&P 500 that generated accounting losses in 2015 were found to have reported profits "on an adjusted basis" after corrections for these non-recurring items.

Is there anything wrong with this picture? Well, in my opinion, not necessarily.

Accounting rules are just that – accounting rules. Many companies actually operate their businesses using internal metrics that might focus more on cash flow or recurring revenues or run-rate performance. This is not to diminish the need for disclosure of GAAP-compliant financial statements. But if something is truly non-recurring, perhaps like a non-cash goodwill impairment charge or a hefty legal settlement, those things at least deserve consideration for exclusion when thinking about ongoing earning power. One has to be careful, however. As Chris Mercer often says, "business life is full of one non-recurring event after another."

The inclusion of metrics like adjusted EBITDA (arguably the most popular non-GAAP measure) can be helpful to analysts and investors, but only when accompanied by the discrete adjustments used by management to arrive at such a figure. As recently noted by venture capitalist Fred Wilson, "[this] is not spinning. [It] is transparency and it is good." [2]

Even the FASB has commented that having two sets of information can be a powerful analytical tool in understanding the underlying business.[3] To address this issue, the FASB's Financial Performance Reporting Project aims to evaluate ways to improve the relevance of information presented in the performance statement. In April, the SEC also voted to solicit public comments on modernizing certain business and financial disclosure requirements in Regulation S-K.[4] We will continue to monitor the development of these initiatives.

End Notes

[1] Available online: http://www.nytimes.com/2016/04/24/business/fantasy-math-is-helping-companies-spin-losses-into-profits.html

[2] Available online: http://avc.com/2016/04/generally-accepted-accounting-standards-gaap/

[3] "For the Investor: The Use of Non-GAAP Metrics", December 2014, http://www.fasb.org

[4] "SEC Solicits Public Comment on Business and Financial Disclosure Requirements in Regulation S-K", April 15, 2016, https://www.sec.gov/news/pressrelease/2016-70.html

Non-GAAP Measures are Gaining Popularity in IPOs

Karolina Calhoun, CPA/ABV
Originally Published on January 16, 2015

Non-GAAP performance measures are becoming more and more popular, particularly for companies looking to raise capital in an IPO. Although financial statements prepared in accordance with GAAP provide the public a standardized basis for historical and comparable financial statements, the use of non-GAAP measures, such as adjusted EBITDA or adjusted gross profit, can allow management to emphasize alternative measures. Non-GAAP performance measures offer companies an opportunity to provide users a better understanding of the company's performance and financial statements as well as management perspectives. After the Sarbanes-Oxley Act of 2002, non-GAAP measures were strictly monitored and rarely used in financial statements. Issued in 2003, Regulation G required that companies which present non-GAAP measures define the basis of the calculation and reconcile the measure to the most relevant GAAP measure. Full disclosure explaining the usefulness and purposes for inclusion is also required. More recently, regulators appear to be becoming less skeptical of non-GAAP measures as more companies and investors rely on non-GAAP measures as a means of understanding and analyzing companies.

In October 2014, PricewaterhouseCoopers published a study on non-GAAP measures used in over 400 IPOs between 2011 and 2013.[1] The study found that approximately 60% of IPOs used at least one non-GAAP measurement. The analysis found that the most commonly used measure was EBITDA, used by

Figure 2.1: Recent IPOs With Non-GAAP Performance Measures

Company	Amt. ($mil)	Date	Non-GAAP Measure	Description of Non-GAAP Measure
On Deck Capital, Inc (ONDK)	$200	12/17/14	Adjusted EBITDA	Excludes interest expense, income tax expense, depreciation & amortization, stock-based compensation expense and warrant liability fair value adjustment.
Rice Midstream Partners, LP (RMP)	$416	12/17/14	Adjusted EBITDA	EBITDA adjusted for stock compensation expense and incentive unit expense.
Metaldyne Performance Group, Inc (MPG)	$150	12/12/14	Adjusted EBITDA & Adjusted Free Cash Flow	Adjusted for certain material non-cash items and unusual items not expected to continue into the future.
Hortonworks, Inc (HDP)	$100	12/12/14	Gross billings	Revenue plus the change in deferred revenue during period.
James River Group Holdings, Ltd (JRVR)	$231	12/12/14	Net operating income	Excludes net realized investment gains/losses, due diligence costs for M&A activities, severance costs, impairment charges on goodwill and intangible assets, gains on extinguishment of debt and interest expense.
LendingClub Corp (LC)	$866	12/11/14	Contribution, Contribution margin	Net income/loss excluding net interest income/expense and other adjustments, general and administrative expense, stock-based compensation expense and income tax expense/benefit.
Neff Corp (NEFF)	$157	11/21/14	EBITDA and Adjusted EBITDA	EBITDA adjusted for relative risk of investment in securities.
CNOVA N.V. (CNV)	$188	11/20/14	1) Adjusted EBITDA, 2) Free cash flow	1) EBITDA adjusted for restructuring, IPO expenses, litigation, gain/loss from disposal of non-current assets, impairment of assets and share based payments. 2) Adjusted for capital expenditures and factoring expense.
EHI Car Services, Ltd (EHIC)	$120	11/18/14	Adjusted EBITDA	EBITDA adjusted for share-based compensation, interest expenses & income and provision for income taxes.
Virgin America, Inc (VA)	$307	11/14/14	EBITDA and EBITDAR	EBITDAR excludes aircraft rent.

Source: Company S-1 filings, Mercer Capital analysis

over 65% of the IPOs analyzed. Further, of these IPOs presenting EBITDA, 46% also presented adjusted EBITDA. The adjustments included equity-based compensation, impairments, expenses related to acquisitions, restructuring and reorganization, non-recurring & unusual charges, and gain/loss on foreign exchange currency.

A look at more recent IPOs confirms the popularity of non-GAAP measures.

As shown in Figure 2.1, Mercer Capital reviewed ten recent IPOs that each raised in excess of $100 million. Adjusted EBITDA continues to be the most commonly used non-GAAP measure. However, each company may define Adjusted EBITDA differently, which creates problems when investors and analysts attempt to track and benchmark companies over time and to each other. So while non-GAAP measures might make for a shorthand way to communicate results, they are no replacement for sound financial analysis when it comes to valuation.

End Note

[1]   Available online: http://www.pwc.com/us/en/deals/publications/assets/non-gaap.pdf

3

Our Economy Has Changed. Should Our Accounting Standards?

Taryn E. Burgess
Originally Published on April 11, 2016

Companies are allocating more money to developing nonphysical assets such as databases and brands than to building physical assets, such as new factories. With the rise of technology and professional service firms, which generate ideas and provide knowledge-based services rather than physical assets, the U.S. marketplace is shifting from one which supplies goods to one which supplies ideas. The U.S. generates a large share of wealth from intangible assets such as patents, copyrights, and business processes. This store of value is essentially invisible to investors because internally generated intangible assets are not reported on the balance sheet. There is a growing gap in the balance sheet reflecting this shift from physical assets to intangible ideas and the Financial Accounting Standards Board (FASB) is even considering adding the topic to its rule making agenda.

Under current accounting rules, companies only record acquired intangible assets on their balance sheet, because acquisition accounting requires that a purchaser allocate the consideration paid among all asset (tangible and intangible). It is not a new idea that intangible assets have worth. Macroeconomic theory asserts that technological change increases factor total-factor productivity, and therefore GDP, over the long term. But accounting principles are not necessarily required to adhere to economic theory.

Figure 3.1

Arguments For	Arguments Against
Significance to the Economy Intangible assets are becoming increasingly significant to our economy. The Wall Street Journal estimated that altogether, U.S. Companies have more than \$8 trillion in intangible assets, which is nearly half the combined market capitalization of the S&P 500. An asset base measured solely on tangible assets is inadequate to explain/support a company's current and future cash generating potential.	**Time Consuming and Expensive** Companies already spend weeks preparing for audits and the addition of intangible to the balance sheet may increase this time and make the process even more costly. Small public companies already feel the costs associated with financial reporting standards and some opponents suggest that increasing the requirements may lead to compliance costs that outweigh the benefits of being a public firm.
Gauging Risks In order to properly gauge risk an investor can evaluate the balance sheet to understand the source of cash flows. In a well-functioning market, creditworthy borrowers can obtain funds in order to grow. But many professional service firms, technology firms, and startups have few tangible assets and may appear to be a more risky investment than they truly are. Would markets be more efficient with an informationally-complete balance sheet?	**Limited Worth** Some have questioned the benefits of such added disclosures, suggesting that fund managers and other investors do not place significant weight on the balance sheet in the first place when making investment decisions. The value of internally generated intangibles could be viewed as simply the difference between a company's market capitalization and its book value. Thus, why should companies have to spend the time and effort classifying their intangibles and assigning them?

In 2013, the Bureau of Economic Analysis (BEA) changed the way it calculated Gross Domestic Product (GDP) in order to capture the changing nature of the economy. The BEA reclassified research and development costs as investments, similar to the costs of building a factory, and they reclassified original works of art as long-lived assets. They reasoned that being able to effectively measure the role of research and such activities in the US economy would promote innovation. GDP is the yard-stick for our macro-economy, and the BEA argued that it is "better to be imprecisely correct than precisely incorrect."

This would not be the first time that the FASB has considered adding internally-generated intangibles to the balance sheet. Previously they were unable to resolve the issue of how companies would value intangibles; would it be based on fair value or cost? But, as previously mentioned, valuation specialists and consulting firms routinely measure the fair value of such assets, most often in the context of acquisition accounting and for bankruptcy purposes.

Valuation methods fall into one of three approaches: cost, market, or income. While a lack of sufficient data on comparable assets can make the market approach difficult in some industries, the cost approach and income approach are more often used to value intangible assets.

Valuation under the cost approach requires estimation of the cost to replace the subject asset, as well as opportunity costs in the form of cash flows foregone as the replacement is sought or recreated. The income approach involves estimating the amount of cash flow produced annually by the subject asset, projecting those cash flows out over the expected life of the asset, and selecting an appropriate discount rate to determine the present value of the future benefits.

Ultimately, in order for the accounting community to reach a decision regarding the accounting for intangible asset, the purpose of the balance sheet may have to be reconsidered. The balance sheet currently serves as a record of cost and subsequent reductions in the values of (mostly tangible) assets. But, if the intended purpose of a balance sheet were to become an accounting for all of the income-generating assets of the firm, then clearly a new set of accounting standards would be required. This is a big issue, and one that would have considerable ramifications for existing practice and reporting. Nevertheless, the FASB is thinking about it – and so should stakeholders.

4

PCAOB to Focus on M&A and Fair Value in 2016

Lucas Parris, CFA, ASA-BV/IA
Originally Published on August 15, 2016

In July 2016, the PCAOB issued a staff inspection brief to provide information about the plan, scope and objectives of PCAOB inspections in 2016 of registered audit firms and their audits of issuers.[1] Translation: watch out for these potential landmines when preparing, auditing, or reviewing your firm's financial statements.

The 2016 guidance comes on the heels of an April 2016 brief that gave a preview of observations from the PCAOB's 2015 inspection cycle.[2] In that report, the most frequent audit deficiencies continue to be related to:

- Internal control over financial reporting

- Assessing and responding to risks of material misstatement

- Auditing accounting estimates, including fair value measurements

The PCAOB has previously stated that accounting estimates usually warrant more audit attention because they often involve complex methods, including models, subjective factors, and judgments, which make them susceptible to management bias.

The audit deficiencies most frequently identified during the 2015 inspection cycle included:

- Testing estimates arising from the valuation of assets and liabilities acquired in a business combination (ASC 805)

- Evaluating impairment analyses for goodwill and other long-lived assets (ASC 350 and 360)

- Other less frequent deficiencies included those relating to financial instruments, revenue-related estimates and reserves, allowances for loan losses, inventory reserves, and tax-related estimates.

Some of these topics are [unfortunately] of no surprise to those that have followed the evolution of fair value accounting. In a recent issue of the *Harvard Business Review*, in an article entitled "Where Financial Reporting Still Falls Short," authors David Sherman and David Young cite the difficulties in applying fair value principles consistently to value intangible assets. The HBR piece also comments on the lack of useful disclosures regarding of how such assets are valued and what assumptions were made in generating fair value estimates. Even on this blog, we've documented these deficiencies numerous times.

Ongoing concern about the broadening application of fair value measurement and a perceived lack of consistency in the valuation work product has even led to development of a new shared professional credential by the American Institute of Certified Public Accountants (AICPA), American Society of Appraisers (ASA), and the Royal Institution of Chartered Surveyors (RICS).

But back to the issue at hand—what will the PCAOB focus on in 2016? As always, the PCAOB begins with audit areas where deficiencies have been identified in previous inspection cycles. There will also be a consideration of areas potentially affected by current economic factors. One of these factors is the effect of increasing M&A activity on fair value measurement auditing. The Staff Inspection Brief notes the following risk areas:

- Increasing transaction activity may increase the risk of improper valuation of assets acquired and liabilities assumed given larger deal sizes

- Heightened risk of improper valuation due to greater transaction complexity

- Risks of material misstatement associated with the proper identification of all intangible assets

- Improper assignment of goodwill to reporting units

- Risk of misstatements in connection with contingent consideration fair value measurements

The PCAOB staff also noted that fair value measurements involve the potential for management bias, and that in many cases auditors have not historically applied an appropriate degree of professional skepticism when testing estimates. As an example, the inspections staff observed instances in which auditors did not sufficiently evaluate or consider contradictory or potentially inconsistent information. Of course, greater PCAOB scrutiny eventually flows down to preparers of financial statements in the form of more comprehensive examination (and questions) from the auditors regarding these issues. In our own practice, we have witnessed increased auditor willingness to delve deeper into the assumptions underlying fair value estimates as well as management's support for prospective financial information. As valuation specialists that regularly provide fair value measurements, we at Mercer Capital completely understand these concerns because best practices pertaining to professional skepticism and analytical judgment apply to us, too.

End Notes

[1] Available online: https://pcaobus.org/Inspections/Documents/Inspection-Brief-2016-3-Issuers.pdf

[2] Available online: https://pcaobus.org/Inspections/Documents/Inspection-Brief-2016-1-Auditors-Issuers.pdf

5

In the Eye of the Beholder: Increasing SEC Scrutiny of Public Company Fair Value Marks

Samantha L. Albert

Originally Published on September 21, 2015

In August 2015, NERA Economic Consulting examined some of the effects of the SEC's increasing use of quantitative analysis to identify potential problematic valuations in public company filings. Although the SEC previously used its tools in the private fund advisor sphere, the agency is beginning to turn its gaze to publicly traded companies. Thus far, the SEC's focus has been on two main points, valuation policies that differ from actual valuation practices (including valuation methods and approaches, as well as the inputs used) and the incorporation of market conditions (or lack thereof).

The SEC's tools have so far been successful at flagging unusual or suspect valuations in the private equity, mutual fund, and hedge fund arena, resulting in several enforcement actions:

- **KCAP Financial, Inc.** (2013) This matter was the SEC's first enforcement action against a public company that failed to properly apply fair value principles (referred to as SFAS 157 in 2008). The SEC settled charges against three executives based on the alleged overstatement of the value of debt securities and CDOs. The company executives paid $125,000 in penalties.[1]

- **GLG Partners LP** (2013) The SEC settled charges based on the alleged overvaluation of an emerging market coal company, which subsequently artificially increased fee revenue. GLG and its former holding company paid nearly $9 million in penalties, interest, and repayment.[2]

- **ThinkStrategy Capital Management LLC** (2013) The SEC settled charges against the hedge fund's manager based on the alleged over-statement of assets, misrepresentation of the firm's history, the under-statement of volatility, and the misrepresentation of credentials over a period of seven years. ThinkStrategy and the fund's manager were ordered to pay nearly $5 million in penalties and repayments.[3]

- **Millennium Global Emerging Credit Fund** (ongoing) The SEC charged the Fund's portfolio manager with overstating the fund's returns and net asset value and using fictional prices for two of the fund's illiquid holdings. Although the matter is still ongoing, the port-folio manager was sentenced to four years in prison and was ordered to pay over $390 million in restitution.[4]

In the KCAP matter, management of the company believed that the Level 2 price inputs available for the debt securities in question reflected distressed transactions and instead elected to use an "enterprise value methodology" to value the securities. By using a less visible input and implementing an atypical valuation method, KCAP opened itself to deeper scrutiny from the SEC. The agency alleged that KCAP did not adequately describe and disclose its valuation techniques, resulting in an overvaluation of the subject securities.

As put forth in ASC 820, there are three types of inputs in the fair value hierarchy:

- **Level 1** inputs are directly observable in an active market with unad-justed prices. In general, market transactions are typically seen as the best indication of an asset's value.

- **Level 2** inputs are based on inactive market prices for the subject asset, active market prices for similar assets, or pricing models with Level 1 inputs.

- **Level 3** inputs are unobservable (i.e., not derived from the market).

In general, valuation specialists should use directly observable inputs whenever possible. For example, if the specialist had the option of using a Level 1 or a

Level 3 input, the specialist should choose to use the Level 1 input. If, for some reason, the specialist elects to not use a lower level input, the rationale for doing so and the valuation techniques used must be disclosed, lest the company incur the wrath of the SEC. Certain circumstances that would lead a valuation specialist to choose another input level are typically specific to the asset, but in all cases should reflect the assumptions of market participants for the subject asset. These factors apply regardless of whether the asset in question is a debt security or an illiquid equity holding in a portfolio company.

As the SEC ramps up its use of quantitative analytics and increasingly examines public company fair value measurements, following valuation best practices and disclosing the appropriate information will be increasingly important.

End Notes

[1]   Available online: http://www.sec.gov/News/PressRelease/Detail/PressRelease/1365171486286

[2]   Available online: http://www.sec.gov/News/PressRelease/Detail/PressRelease/1370540491613

[3]   Available online: https://www.sec.gov/litigation/litreleases/2013/lr22588.htm

[4]   Available online: http://www.reuters.com/article/us-usa-crime-balboa-idUSKB-N0EY2C520140623

Business or Asset: Can You Tell the Difference?

Samantha L. Albert
Originally Published on March 7, 2016

"I'm not a businessman, I'm a business, man!"

– Jay-Z

The Financial Accounting Standards Board's (FASB) definition of a business is important when it comes to classifying assets and related expenses. If the target of an acquisition is classified as a business, the acquiring company is required to recognize acquisition expenses immediately as well as measure the fair value of all assets acquired (including goodwill and intangible assets). If the acquisition is classified as a group of assets instead, the acquiring company can capitalize the acquisition expenses and a purchase price allocation would not be required. However, some feel that the FASB's current definition is ambiguous and can result in inconsistent designations of business or asset status.

In November 2015, the FASB proposed a standards update to clarify the assets versus business debate. Under the existing definition included in ASC 805, a "set of assets and activities" is considered a business if it has three characteristics – inputs (intangible assets, IP, access to materials or employees), processes (systems that "have the ability to create outputs"), and outputs (goods, services, revenue, or investment income).[1] However, a set is not required to have outputs to be defined as a business. Additionally, ASC 805 does not set minimum standards as to what constitutes inputs and processes, and potentially allowed for a set to be classified as a business even if processes needed to be supplied or replaced by the acquirer. Together, it has been suggested that these issues complicated companies' abilities to distinguish their acquisitions with certainty.

Under the proposed revision as laid out in the exposure draft, an evaluation of the acquirer's ability to create outputs or replace missing inputs or processes would not be required, and the set would be evaluated on an as-is basis.[2] Rather than looking at the set's ability to produce outputs when combined with the acquirer's existing resource, the revised ASC 805 would consider the set's production of outputs on its own. The revised rule would place more weight on the "reasonable judgment" of the parties involved and its aim is to result in more consistent definitions of business and asset acquisitions.

In practice, if the revised rule is adopted by the FASB, the financial reporting burden for acquiring companies could be reduced. CFOs would have an easier time classifying their acquisitions, potentially leading to savings of both time and expense. The ability to capitalize expenses and delay recognition of transaction costs would certainly be more favorable to near-term earnings. However, the degree to which this change impacts companies is obviously tied to the frequency with which the issue arises in the first place. In our experience, most asset acquisitions occur with respect to purchases of standalone intellectual property (such as a piece of software or a patent), a collection of customer or supplier contracts (without the requisite employees or business processes), or a piece of machinery or equipment.

End Notes

[1]   Available online: http://www.fasb.org/cs/ContentServer?c=Document_C&pagename=FASB%2FDocument_C%2FDocumentPage&cid=1176167643558

[2]   Available online: http://www.fasb.org/jsp/FASB/Document_C/DocumentPage?cid=1176167640849&acceptedDisclaimer=true

Premature Obituaries and Other Mixed Signals

Travis W. Harms, CFA, CPA/ABV
Originally Published on August 15, 2014

Asked to define "ambivalence," one wag reportedly replied, "I suppose it's a bit like watching your mother-in-law drive your brand new Porsche off a cliff – you're just not sure how to feel." Accounting observers following the long and winding road to convergence of FASB and IASB accounting standards will be forgiven for experiencing a similar degree of cognitive dissonance in recent weeks.

First came the obituary. IASB Chairman Hans Hoogervorst seemed to pronounce convergence efforts, which have been ongoing for over a decade, dead during the question and answer session following a speech in late July: "The FASB decided to stick to current American practices and leave the converged position. It's a pity. Convergence would have allowed the U.S. to make the ultimate jump to IFRS. But nobody can force it to do so; if it wants to stick with U.S. GAAP, that's its choice. But IFRS moves on – we have a large part of the world to take care of." [1]

Given the glacial pace of accounting standards setting, inaction on the part of the SEC with regard to accepting IFRS-based financials from U.S. filers, and the struggles to find common ground on key accounting issues such as impairment of financial instruments, it had become clear to most that convergence would be neither easy nor quick. But until Chairman Hoogervorst's comments, no one in a position of authority had sounded the death knell for the project.

A week or so later came the confirming evidence, as the two boards announced that the long-awaited lease accounting standards – one of the most significant of the "convergence" projects – is nearing completion, but will not be "converged." While the FASB has elected to retain a dual model in which some leases will continue to effectively receive traditional operating lease treatment, the IASB has opted for a single model in which all lease agreements are treated as financing transactions.

But then came word that the obituary was, after all, premature. In a speech in Johannesburg, South Africa, the vice-chair of the IASB, Ian Mackintosh, pronounced a single set of global accounting standards "desirable, achievable, and … inevitable." [2]

So, which is it? Is convergence dead, or is it inevitable? We don't know. However, we note that one of the most noteworthy convergence success stories relates to valuation. In 2011, the IASB and FASB issued standards harmonizing the measurement and disclosure of fair value. IFRS 13 and ASC 820 provide a single comprehensive base of guidance for fair value measurements. As a result, while the two accounting standards do not always use fair value in the same way, they do define it in the same way.

End Notes

[1] Available online: http://www.accountingtoday.com/blogs/debits-credits/accounting-convergence-unachievable-71597-1.html?zkPrintable=true

[2] Available online: http://www.cgma.org/magazine/news/pages/201410739.aspx?TestCookiesEnabled=redirect

Lower Valuations for Private Companies?

Karolina Calhoun, CPA/ABV
Originally Published on June 12, 2015

The CFA Institute recently released a report about investor apprehensions concerning separate accounting standards for private companies.[1] The report reflects the results of a survey of investment professionals in the CFA Institute. The separate accounting standards include differing accounting rules for SMEs (small or medium sized entities) under IFRS and for private companies under GAAP (as advanced by the Private Company Council). On balance, while investors seem to think the initiative will reduce companies' compliance costs, they believe the benefits are unlikely to outweigh the costs.

When asked about the impact of private company accounting standards, the results of the survey indicated the following:

- 82% believe comparability between private and public companies would be jeopardized

- 65% said the standards would result in the loss of information typically useful in financial analysis

- 73% said the new standard would generate greater complexity for investors

The CFA Institute report noted:

> *"Establishing separate standards for non-public companies will add complexity and cost to other dimensions of financial reporting. For example, differential accounting standards will make it more costly for users to understand, standards setters to develop and maintain, educators to teach, and assurance providers to obtain proficiency in financial reporting."*

A specific instance of added complexity and costs would be for a private company preparing to go public, or if a public company is interested in acquiring a private company. In both of these cases, the financial statements would not be comparable and the private company would incur time and costs to translate historical financial statements to public company accounting standards.

Investors are also worried about the quality of financial statements under a private company version of GAAP. The requirements for footnote disclosure are likely to be less rigid; specifically, less quantification in favor of more qualitative description. The majority of those polled (78%) agreed that investors would perceive private company accounting standards to be of lower quality than regular U.S. GAAP.

The study also suggests that the loss of information resulting from private company accounting standards may actually lead to lower valuations for private companies. When assessing the value of a firm, investors consider a firm's lack of transparency in different ways, including adjusting the cash flows, discount rate, or expected growth rate. The report suggests that the loss of decision-useful information "will likely lead to an increase in risk premium and cost of capital for non-public companies."

Will the use of alternative accounting standards actually impact private company valuations? That remains to be seen. But a lack of transparency regarding one's investment is certainly a valid rationale for applying a bit more skepticism in valuation.

End Note

[1] Available online: https://blogs.cfainstitute.org/marketintegrity/2015/05/05/study-first-to-give-investor-views-on-complexity-in-corporate-financial-reporting/

Impairment Testing

Five Variations on a Theme: Analyzing Transaction Premium Data

Travis W. Harms, CFA, CPA/ABV
Originally Published on August 1, 2016 and August 8, 2016

The consistent theme of the Appraisal Foundation's exposure draft *The Measurement and Application of Market Participant Acquisition Premiums* is that acquirers do not value control for its own sake, but rather for the tangible economic benefits that can be achieved by the exercise of control. In other words, control of a business enterprise is valuable only to the extent that at least one of two conditions prevail: (1) the control buyer anticipates that the business will generate incremental cash flows under their stewardship, and (2) the control buyer has access to less expensive capital than the current owners.

A logical extension of this theme is that market participant acquisition premiums (or, control premiums, as they have traditionally been known) are more properly conceived of as *outputs* of a valuation process focused on cash flow, risk and growth than as *inputs* used to derive a valuation indication for a controlling interest. As a result, averages or medians of published studies of observed control premium data do not constitute direct valuation evidence. This caution should not be interpreted as belittling the usefulness of such data. Adopting an incremental economic benefits approach to measuring the fair value of controlling interests does not mean that practitioners should drop their subscriptions to *Mergerstat Review*. It does, however, mean that practitioners should consider using the *Mergerstat Review* differently, as suggested in the exposure draft:

"The Working Group cautions that exclusive reliance on observed transaction premium data provides, in most case, insufficient support for a concluded MPAP. Nonetheless, observed transaction premium data may be valuable. The Working Group believes that observed historical premiums provide potentially relevant (albeit indirect) evidence of the appropriate magnitude of the incremental economic benefits anticipated by market participants. The observed premiums can be used to corroborate (or question) the reasonableness of the cash flow forecasts and discount rates underlying fair value measurements within the income approach. However, exclusive reliance on observed transaction premiums without careful analysis of the subject entity's relative financial performance, valuation multiples, and other metrics can result in an unreliable fair value measurement." [1]

Here we will illustrate how observed transaction premiums from the most recent edition of Mergerstat Review can be useful in measuring the fair value of controlling interests.

Summary of the Data

The 2016 edition of *Mergerstat Review* identifies 405 acquisitions of publicly held sellers announced in 2015. The transactions involved companies in 41 different industries. For the 362 transactions with non-negative observed premiums, the average and median premiums were 48.1% and 29.6%, respectively. In the decade ending with 2015, median premiums by year ranged from a low of 23.1% in 2006 to 39.8% in 2009.

The dispersion of actual observations during the year was pronounced, with over 30% of transactions having observed premiums of less than 20%, while observed premiums exceeded 60% in nearly 20% of the transactions.

Given the dispersion evident in Chart 9.1, it should be evident that the median or average observation is of little direct relevance to a specific fair value measurement. Additional analysis is required to draw meaningful conclusions from the data.

The first step is to narrow the scope of analysis to the relevant industry. For the purpose of this post, we will examine the data for the retail industry. *Mergerstat*

Chart 9.1: 2015 Observed Premiums

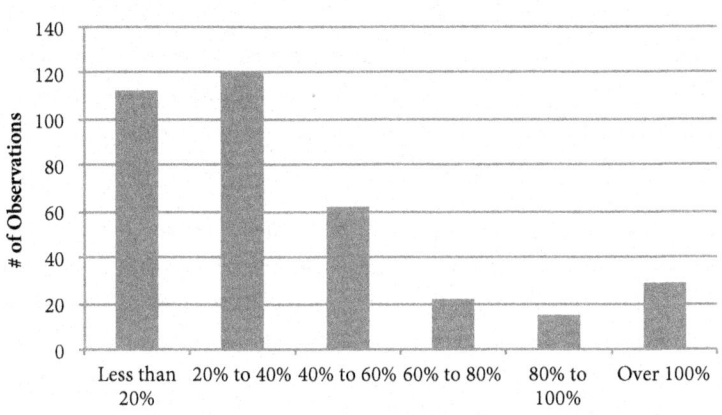

Figure 9.1: 2015 Retail Transactions

Deal	Seller	Announce Date	Share Prices Pre-Announce	Transaction	Reported Premium
1	Steiner Leisure	8/21/15	$58.39	$65.00	11.3%
2	Omnicare, Inc.	5/21/15	91.81	98.00	6.7%
3	Rite-Aid Corp.	10/27/15	6.33	9.00	42.2%
4	Roundy's, Inc.	11/11/15	2.25	3.60	60.0%
5	Books-A-Million, Inc.	1/29/15	1.68	3.25	92.3%
6	ANN, Inc.	5/18/15	38.99	46.91	20.6%
7	Liberator Medical Holdings, Inc.	11/20/15	2.63	3.35	27.4%
8	zulily, Inc.	8/17/15	13.48	18.61	39.1%
	Median				**33.3%**
	Average				**37.5%**

Source: Mergerstat Review, SEC filings, Mercer Capital analysis

Review identifies 10 transactions in the retail industry during 2015 involving public sellers. Excluding one foreign transaction and one transaction that was cancelled prior to closing, we analyzed the remaining eight transactions.

The median and average discounts for the group are generally comparable to the aggregate measures reviewed previously. As with the overall data set, the dispersion of observed premiums for the retail transactions is quite wide, ranging from 6.7% to 92.3%.

One of the most practical best practices recommended in the Exposure Draft is that premiums be expressed using invested capital or enterprise value as the denominator, rather than equity. This recommendation reflects the emphasis on *enterprise-level cash flow*, risk, and growth as the principal factors influencing the magnitude of an observed transaction premium. For traditional data sources such as *Mergerstat Review*, this necessitates conversion of the equity premiums to an enterprise basis.

Since the control premium is actually a dollar amount (the difference between minority and control values), using a larger denominator (enterprise value) deflates the percentage premiums relative to the traditional equity basis percentages.[2] The median and average premiums on an enterprise value basis are 21.3% and 23.4%, respectively, and the range of observed premiums has contracted appreciably (5.6% to 46.8%).

The analyst's task at this point is to consider whether further insights can be extracted from the data. As we will demonstrate in the remaining sections of this report, the transactions in Figure 9.2 illustrate five common variations on the incremental economic benefits theme.

Variation #1: Industry Consolidation

The most common motivating factor for control buyers in our sample is consolidation. By acquiring a company in the same industry, the control buyer anticipates some degree of cost savings, such that the cash flows from the acquired business following the transaction will be greater than the cash flows expected by the pre-transaction minority shareholders.[3]

Figure 9.2: 2015 Retail Transactions

Deal	Seller	Reported Equity Premium	Minority Enterprise Value	Control Enterprise Value	Enterprise Value Premium
1	Steiner Leisure	11.3%	$809.8	$894.6	10.5%
2	Omnicare, Inc.	6.7%	10,681.1	11,280.8	5.6%
3	Rite-Aid Corp.	42.2%	13,856.2	16,648.0	20.1%
4	Roundy's, Inc.	60.0%	760.8	827.5	8.8%
5	Books-A-Million, Inc.	92.3%	53.2	76.7	44.1%
6	ANN, Inc.	20.6%	1,616.9	1,981.1	22.5%
7	Liberator Medical Holdings, Inc.	27.4%	133.0	171.5	29.0%
8	zulily, Inc.	39.1%	1,356.3	1,991.5	46.8%
	Median	**33.3%**	**$1,083.1**	**$1,437.8**	**21.3%**
	Average	**37.5%**	**$3,658.4**	**$4,234.0**	**23.4%**

Source: Mergerstat Review, SEC filings, Mercer Capital analysis

Figure 9.3: Industry Consolidation Transactions

Deal	Seller	Buyer	Enterprise Value Premium
1	Steiner Leisure	Catterton Management Co	10.5%
2	Omnicare, Inc.	CVS Health Corp	5.6%
3	**Rite-Aid Corp.**	**Walgreens Boots Alliance**	**20.1%**
4	**Roundy's, Inc.**	**The Kroger Co**	**8.8%**
5	Books-A-Million, Inc.	BAM Management Group	44.1%
6	**ANN, Inc.**	**Ascena Retail Group**	**22.5%**
7	Liberator Medical Holdings, Inc.	C.R. Bard, Inc.	29.0%
8	zulily, Inc.	Liberty Interactive Corp.	46.8%

Source: Mergerstat Review, SEC filings, Mercer Capital analysis

In each case, the buyer is considerably larger than the seller, and was trading at a higher multiple of EBITDA than the seller prior to the transaction.

The Kroger acquisition of Roundy's illustrates many of the concepts relevant to industry consolidation transactions. At the transaction date, Roundy's operated 150 grocery stores in Wisconsin and Illinois. Kroger operates over 2,750 grocery stores in 35 states. Figure 9.4 summarizes pertinent comparative data for Kroger and Roundy's at the transaction date.

Prior to the transaction, Kroger reported an EBITDA margin of 5.2% and was trading at an EBITDA multiple of 9.0x, compared to an EBITDA margin and multiple of 2.6% and 7.1x, respectively, for Roundy's. In addition, Roundy's had significant financial leverage. As a result, what appears to be a large control premium as reported in *Mergerstat* (60.0%) is only 8.8% on an enterprise value basis. The transaction price implies an enterprise value of 7.8x EBITDA.

The difference in EBITDA margin suggests that Kroger may anticipate implementing cost saving measures that will improve Roundy's margins on a *pro forma* basis. Assuming that the transaction multiple of pro forma EBITDA is equal to the pre-transaction seller multiple, the transaction price implies a *pro forma* EBITDA margin for Roundy's of 2.9%, or approximately 30 basis points higher than the historical margin, and still well below Kroger's consolidated margin.

One can also speculate as to the synergistic value of Roundy's to Kroger by applying Kroger's own EBITDA multiple to a measure of *pro forma* EBITDA that is closer to Kroger's margin, as shown in the rightmost column in Figure 9.4. This synergistic value is not equal to fair value, but does illustrate the potential value range over which market participants would negotiate in arriving at a transaction price. The point over that range at which the transaction price settles will reflect the relative negotiating positions of the two parties. In this case, Kroger's larger scale and superior margins, combined with Roundy's precarious financial condition suggested that Kroger had the upper hand in negotiations and therefore retained the majority of the incremental value created by the transaction. Given the potential value range of $761 million (marketable minority) to $1.63 billion (synergistic value), the transaction price of $827 million apportions most of the incremental

Figure 9.4: Analysis of Kroger Acquisition of Roundy's

| | Kroger | Roundy's | | | |
		Minority	Control	Pro Forma	Synergistic
LTM Revenue	$108,872	$4,028	$4,028	$4,028	$4,028
LTM EBITDA	$5,608	$107	$107	$117	$181
Margin	5.2%	2.6%	2.6%	2.9%	4.5%
Shares O/S	1,066.0	49.4	49.4	49.4	49.4
times: Pre-Announce Price	$37.01	$2.25	$3.60	$3.60	$20.01
Equity Market Capitalization	$39,453	$111	$178	$178	$988
plus: Interest-Bearing Debt	11,259	646	646	646	646
plus: Noncontrolling Interest	(26)	0	0	0	0
less: Cash	(274)	(33)	(33)	(33)	(33)
less: Investments	0	36	36	36	36
Enterprise Value	$50,412	$761	$827	$827	$1,631
Net Debt / EBITDA	2.0x	5.8x	5.8x	5.3x	3.4x
EV / Revenue	0.46x	0.19x	0.21x	0.21x	0.41x
EV / EBITDA	9.0x	7.1x	7.8x	7.1x	9.0x

benefits to the buyer. Nonetheless, given the significant financial leverage, the premium to Roundy's common shareholders from the transaction was substantial.

As shown in Figure 9.5, similar analysis can be applied to the Rite Aid and ANN transactions.

The Rite-Aid narrative is quite similar to the Roundy's/Kroger transaction. Walgreens (the buyer) was larger, had a more attractive EBITDA margin, and was awarded a higher valuation multiple than Rite-Aid (the seller), which was also in a weaker financial position (net debt at 5.8x EBITDA). However, Rite-Aid did enjoy a better relative negotiating position than Roundy's, given its greater scale. Although smaller than Walgreen's, there are few potential targets that would be as material to Walgreens. As a result, Rite-Aid was able to extract a greater portion of the potential value range than Roundy's.[4]

Figure 9.5: Analysis of Rite-Aid and ANN Transactions

| | Walgreens | Rite Aid | | | |
		Minority	Control	Pro Forma	Synergistic
LTM Revenue	$117,922	$27,853	$27,853	$27,853	$27,853
LTM EBITDA	$8,674	$1,274	$1,274	$1,527.3	$1,810.4
Margin	7.4%	4.6%	4.6%	**5.5%**	**6.5%**
Enterprise Value	$115,538	$13,856	$16,648	$16,648	$24,079
EV / Revenue	0.98x	0.50x	0.60x	0.60x	0.86x
EV / EBITDA	13.3x	10.9x	13.1x	10.9x	13.3x

Note - Revenue and EBITDA figures for Walgreens are forward estimates.

| | Ascena | ANN, Inc. | | | |
		Minority	Control	Pro Forma	Synergistic
LTM Revenue	$4,828	$2,541	$2,541	$2,541	$2,541
LTM EBITDA	$263	$241	$241	$254	**$261**
Margin	5.4%	9.5%	9.5%	**10.0%**	10.3%
Enterprise Value	$2,225	$1,617	$1,981	$1,981	$2,219
EV / Revenue	0.46x	0.64x	0.78x	0.78x	0.87x
EV / EBITDA	8.5x	6.7x	8.2x	7.8x	8.5x

The acquisition of ANN, Inc. by Ascena Retail Group, Inc. differs in a couple respects from the other two transactions. First, the buyer (Ascena Retail Group), while larger, is comparable in size to ANN. Second, ANN's EBITDA margins compare favorably to those of the buyer, suggesting that there is less low-hanging fruit available for margin enhancement. As a result, the spread between the minority and synergistic control values is likely narrower, and the seller was in a relatively strong negotiating position, thereby capturing a greater proportion of the potential incremental value.[5]

Variation #2: Vertical Integration

Liberator Medical Holdings sells medical supplies, including urological catheters, on a direct-to-consumer basis, primarily to Medicare-eligible seniors. Liberator was acquired by C.R. Bard, a multinational developer, manufacturer and

Figure 9.6: Analysis of C.R. Bard Acquisition of Liberator Medical

	Liberator Medical Holdings, Inc.			
	Minority	Control	Pro Forma	Synergistic
LTM Revenue	$81.6	$81.6	$81.6	$81.6
plus: Incremental BCR Revenue			$10.4	$10.4
Pro Forma Revenue			$92.0	$92.0
LTM EBITDA	13.1	13.1	13.1	13.1
plus: Incremental BCR EBITDA			3.7	3.7
Pro Forma EBITDA			16.8	16.8
Liberator Margin	16.0%	16.0%	16.0%	16.0%
C.R. Bard Margin			35.9%	35.9%
Shares O/S	53.6	53.6	53.6	53.6
times: Pre-Announce Price	$2.63	$3.35	$3.35	$3.79
Equity Market Capitalization	$140.9	$179.5	$179.5	$203.0
plus: Interest-Bearing Debt	1.5	1.5	1.5	1.5
plus: Noncontrolling Interest	0.0	0.0	0.0	0.0
less: Cash	(9.4)	(9.4)	(9.4)	(9.4)
less: Investments	0.0	0.0	0.0	0.0
Enterprise Value	$133.0	$171.5	$171.5	$195.1
EV / Revenue	1.63x	2.10x	2.10x	2.39x
EV / EBITDA	10.2x	13.1x	10.2x	11.6x

marketer of medical devices, including urology products such as those sold by Liberator. In contrast to the horizontal consolidation of companies in the same line of business, the acquisition of Liberator Medical by Bard is an example of a business combination as a vertical integration strategy. As a result, the relative margins of the buyer and seller are much less pertinent.

In Figure 9.6, we have developed pro forma and synergistic cases for the Liberator transaction focused on increasing revenue to Bard as a result of the vertical integration.

Assuming no change in the buyer or seller margins, a pro forma EBITDA multiple of 10.2x implies $10.4 million of annual incremental revenue to Bard. Combining this estimate of pro forma EBITDA with Bard's higher valuation multiple yields a potential synergistic enterprise value of $195 million. With robust revenue growth (~11.5% 4-year CAGR) and a growing base of recurring customers, Liberator presented a unique acquisition opportunity. As a result, it was able to extract a majority of the potential incremental value in the transaction.

Variation #3: Diversification

Two of the transactions illustrate acquisitions motivated by the desire to diversify.

- CVS is a pharmacy company, providing both pharmacy benefit management and retail pharmacy services. In May 2015, CVS acquired Omnicare, Inc., a provider of pharmaceuticals and pharmacy services to long-term care facilities and specialty pharmacy and commercialization services for the biopharmaceutical industry.

- zulily, Inc. is an online retailer specializing in "flash" sales. From 2010 through 2014, zulily's revenue grew from $18.4 million to $1.20 billion (a compound annual growth rate of nearly 185%). Liberty Interactive Media, Inc. operates the QVC television shopping network. Over the same period, Liberty's revenue grew at a compound annual rate of 4.6%, reaching $10.5 billion in 2014.

Figure 9.7 summarizes analysis for the Omnicare and zulily transactions. For diversification acquisitions, the cost savings are likely less significant than in consolidation transactions. Prior to the acquisition, Omnicare reported a higher EBITDA margin than CVS and was accorded a higher EBITDA multiple than CVS, suggesting that the primary levers available to support substantial premiums were lacking. Consistent with this observation, the observed premium was just 5.6% on an enterprise value basis (6.7% on an equity basis).

zulily had experienced rapid revenue growth since inception. As evident in the minority and control EBITDA multiples, the value of zulily was influenced by revenue growth potential much more than current profitability. We speculate that a portion of the motivation for Liberty was the expectation of a "halo" effect from the addition of the fast-growing zulily business to its portfolio of assets. Were the combination to add a quarter turn to Liberty's EBITDA multiple, that

Figure 9.7: Analysis of Omnicare and zulily Transactions

	CVS	Omnicare			
		Minority	Control	Pro Forma	Synergistic
LTM Revenue	$143,010	$6,506	$6,506	$6,506	$6,506
LTM EBITDA	$10,851	$752	$752	$794	**$802**
Margin	7.6%	11.6%	11.6%	**12.2%**	12.3%
Enterprise Value	$127,992	$10,681	$11,281	$11,281	$11,388
EV / Revenue	0.89x	1.64x	1.73x	1.73x	1.75x
EV / EBITDA	11.8x	14.2x	15.0x	**14.2x**	**14.2x**

	Liberty Interactive	zulily, Inc.			
		Minority	Control	Pro Forma	Synergistic
LTM Revenue	$10,048	$1,281	$1,281	$1,281	$1,281
LTM EBITDA	$1,852	$29.8	$29.8	$43.8	$43.8
Margin	18.4%	2.3%	2.3%	**3.4%**	**3.4%**
Enterprise Value	$20,518	$1,356	$1,991	$1,991	$2,454
EV / Revenue	2.04x	1.06x	1.55x	1.55x	1.92x
EV / EBITDA	11.1x	45.5x	66.8x	**45.5x**	56.1x

would contribute an additional $463 million to the company's market capitalization, which would help support the 45.8% enterprise value premium paid.[6]

Variation #4: Private Equity Acquisition

Steiner Leisure provides spa and ancillary aesthetic services aboard cruise ships and in other venues, sells beauty products, and operates schools. Steiner was acquired by Catterton Partners, a private equity firm, in a transaction announced in August 2015. Private equity funds are the prototypical financial, as opposed to strategic, buyers.[7]

Figure 9.8 compares the multiples implied by Catterton's purchase to the pre-announcement trading value of Steiner's minority shares. The transaction price implied an EBITDA multiple of 12.1x, compared to 11.0x on a pre-announcement basis.

Figure 9.8: Analysis of Catterton Partners Acquisition of Steiner Leisure

	Minority	Control	Pro Forma	Synergistic
LTM Revenue	$870.9	$870.9	$870.9	$870.9
LTM EBITDA	73.6	73.6	**81.3**	81.0
Margin	8.5%	8.5%	9.3%	**9.3%**
Shares O/S	12.8	12.8	12.8	12.8
times: Pre-Announce Price	$58.39	$65.00	$65.00	**$71.03**
Equity Market Capitalization	$749.0	$833.8	$833.8	$911.2
plus: Interest-Bearing Debt	108.6	108.6	108.6	108.6
plus: Noncontrolling Interest	0.0	0.0		0.0
less: Cash	(47.8)	(47.8)	(47.8)	(47.8)
less: Investments	0.0	0.0	0.0	0.0
Enterprise Value	$809.8	$894.6	$894.6	$971.9
Net Debt / EBITDA	0.8x	0.8x	0.7x	0.8x
EV / Revenue	0.93x	1.03x	1.03x	1.12x
EV / EBITDA	11.0x	12.1x	11.0x	**12.0x**

Figure 9.9: Cost of Capital Analysis

	Minority	Control
Pre-tax Cost of Debt	3.80%	5.00%
less: Taxes	62.0%	62.0%
After-tax Cost of Debt	2.36%	3.10%
Weight	10.0%	40.0%
Risk-free Rate	2.44%	2.44%
plus: Common Stock Premium	5.50%	5.50%
plus: Size Premium	2.04%	2.04%
plus: Specific-Company Risk	**0.00%**	**2.00%**
Total Equity Return	9.98%	11.98%
Weight	90.0%	60.0%
WACC	**9.2%**	**8.4%**

The multiple pick-up in the transaction likely corresponds to a reduction in the weighted average cost of capital on the order of 50 to 100 basis points. Even with the higher costs of debt and equity associated with more leveraged capital structures, the availability of favorable transaction financing can reduce the weighted average cost of capital for an acquirer like Catterton, as illustrated in Figure 9.9.

Relative to the industry consolidation and vertical integration transactions, the enterprise value premium for the private equity transaction (10.5%) is more modest, reflecting the relative significance of financing versus cash flow benefits.

Variation #5: Market Inefficiency

Books-A-Million, Inc. operates 256 bookstores and 42 frozen yogurt shops, primarily in the eastern United States, reporting approximately $475 million of revenue during the fiscal year ended January 31, 2015. Despite being publicly-traded, the directors and executive officers of the company owned nearly 65% of the outstanding shares prior to the transaction. Since suspending dividend payments in 2011, the company's share price fell from around $4.00 to a low of $1.40 per share in late 2014 before recovering modestly to $1.68 prior to the announcement that the Anderson family (founders and controlling shareholders) was proposing to take the company private. At that price, the aggregate market value of the shares held by outsiders was less than $9 million. As shown in Figure 9.10, the pre-transaction share price implied an EBITDA multiple of 2.5x. In sum, there was no compelling reason for the company to be public.

Assuming $1 million of annual cost savings from relief of public reporting requirements, the implied EBITDA multiple from the buyout price was 3.4x. Applying a still-modest lower middle market transaction multiple of 4.5x to pro forma EBITDA yields a synergistic enterprise value of $101 million. Following an initial offer of $2.75 per share, the Anderson family increased its offer to $3.25 per share (a 92% premium to the pre-announcement price) to complete the transaction.

The Books-A-Million transaction illustrates how a substantial observed premium (92% on equity base; 42% on enterprise base) can reflect unusual circumstances surrounding trading in the subject company's shares rather than significant synergistic benefits.

Figure 9.10: Analysis of Books-A-Million Management Buyout

	Minority	Control	Pro Forma	Synergistic
LTM Revenue	$474.1	$474	$474	$474
LTM EBITDA	21.5	21.5	**22.5**	**22.5**
Margin	4.5%	4.5%	4.7%	4.7%
Shares O/S	15.0	15.0	15.0	15.0
times: Pre-Announce Price	$1.68	$3.25	$3.25	**$4.89**
Equity Market Capitalization	$25.1	$48.6	$48.6	$73.2
plus: Interest-Bearing Debt	33.6	33.6	33.6	33.6
plus: Noncontrolling Interest	2.4	2.4		2.4
less: Cash	(5.8)	(5.8)	(5.8)	(5.8)
less: Investments	(2.2)	(2.2)	(2.2)	(2.2)
Enterprise Value	$53.2	$76.7	$76.7	$101.3
Net Debt / EBITDA	1.3x	1.3x	1.2x	1.2x
EV / Revenue	0.11x	0.16x	0.16x	0.21x
EV / EBITDA	2.5x	3.6x	**3.4x**	**4.5x**

Figure 9.11:
Comparison of Variations on the Incremental Economic Benefits Theme

	Primary Benefit	Likely Characteristics
Industry Consolidation	Cost savings	Larger competitors in same line of business with better margins
Vertical Integration	Incremental revenue	Existence of suppliers who could increase volume or customers who could increase margin
Diversification	Cost savings / Multiple expansion	Possess a unique attribute that would reduce perceived risk / augment growth profile of acquirer
Leveraged Buyout	Lower cost of capital	Mature, cash-generating business with optimal operating margins
Market Inefficiency	Eliminate net costs of being public	Small shareholder base, low equity market cap, no analyst coverage, implied multiple below transaction comps

Concluding Thoughts

The recurring theme of the Appraisal Foundation's control premium exposure draft is that transaction premiums are attributable to incremental economic benefits available to the control buyer. Examining observed transaction data for the retail industry from the *2016 Mergerstat Review*, we identified five variations on this theme, as summarized in Figure 9.11.

The fact that the market participant acquisition premium is an output, rather than an input, to a controlling interest fair value measurement does not render observed transaction premium data obsolete. It ought, however, to push valuation specialists to dig deeper into the transactions for which premiums have been observed. Evaluating the observed transactions through the lens of the five variations identified above will allow the analyst to develop a compelling narrative to support market participant assumptions regarding the incremental economic benefits available to a controlling buyer of the subject interest and assess the reasonableness of the resulting market participant acquisition premium.

End Notes

[1] Appraisal Foundation, APB VFR Advisory: The Measurement and Application of Market Participant Acquisition Premiums, exposure draft issued September 1, 2015, page 29, lines 588-597.

[2] The Exposure Draft does not specify whether the debt component of the denominator should be gross or net of cash. In the examples in this post, we have used net debt (i.e., an enterprise value basis). Use of either gross or net debt is consistent with the spirit of the best practices guidance. We have used the enterprise value basis to promote consistency with enterprise value multiples of revenue and EBITDA that we will reference in subsequent sections. When using net debt, companies with cash balances in excess of interest-bearing debt will have enterprise values less than equity values, which will cause the enterprise value premiums to be larger than the equity value premiums (as is the case with ANN, Liberator Medical Holdings, and zulily in Figure 9.2).

[3] Revenue synergies are also possible, but in the case of these transactions, seem less likely than cost savings, so we will focus on the latter.

[4] As of the date of drafting, Rite-Aid shareholders have approved the transaction, but regulatory approval is pending, and the transaction has not yet closed.

[5] That is not to say that management of the acquirer has not identified cost savings. Ascena management indicated potential cost savings of $80 million in an investor

presentation. However, a focus on margin relative to peers can help to maintain a focus on market participant synergies for the acquired business, rather than allowing secondary benefits potentially accruing to the buyer to unduly influence the fair value measurement.

[6]   Or, perhaps, they simply overpaid. That possibility cannot be discounted. Liberty's share price fell from approximately $30 per share to $26 per share in the six weeks following the transaction announcement, and has generally been mired at that level since.

[7]   Most private equity firms do focus on particular segments of the economy. Catterton is no exception, focusing on consumer products and services companies. While operational expertise and the opportunity for cost savings through shared services is a potential source of incremental economic benefit, the opportunity for material margin enhancements is more limited than for strategic buyers.

10

New Rules for Goodwill Impairment?

Lucas Parris, CFA, ASA-BV/IA
Originally Published on October 30, 2015

As the end of the year approaches, many companies are preparing for goodwill impairment testing, which frequently takes place in the fourth quarter. And even with some sectors of the equity markets at near-record highs, the potential for goodwill impairment can still be a very real issue for businesses in certain industries.

It is against this backdrop that the FASB has proposed some changes to the way companies test goodwill for impairment. At a meeting of the FASB on October 28, 2015, the Board discussed whether and how to change the subsequent measurement of goodwill for public companies and not-for-profit entities.[1] These developments are just latest in the nearly two years of discussions on the topic dating back to November of 2013.

The Board has tentatively decided to proceed with the project under a phased approach.

- **Phase 1** – The first phase aims to simplify the goodwill impairment test by removing the requirement to perform a hypothetical purchase price allocation when the carrying value of a reporting unit exceeds its fair value. That analysis is currently referred to as Step 2 of the impairment model under ASC 350. The Board considered but decided not to allow entities an option to perform step 2.

- **Phase 2** – In the second phase of the project, the Board plans to work concurrently with the IASB to address any additional concerns about the subsequent accounting for goodwill.

With respect to not-for-profit entities, the Board decided not to allow not-for-profit entities the accounting alternative currently available to private companies (which includes the amortization of goodwill and a one-step, trigger-based impairment test performed at the entity level or reporting unit level) at this time.

Another area of concern in recent years has been the challenges of performing a goodwill impairment test for reporting units with zero or negative carrying value. In conjunction with the simplified approach to calculating the amount of an impairment charge (elimination of Step 2), the Board decided that if a reporting unit has zero or negative carrying value and it is more likely than not that goodwill is impaired, an entity would be required to write off the full carrying amount of goodwill allocated to that reporting unit. The Board also indicated that it would further analyze the qualitative assessment for entities with reporting units with a zero or negative carrying value. The proposed rules would not affect when companies should consider interim goodwill impairment testing.

End Note

[1] Tentative Board Decisions – October 28, 2015 Meeting. FASB. http://www.fasb.org/cs/ContentServer?c=FASBContent_C&pagename=FASB%2FFASBContent_C%-2FActionAlertPage&cid=1176167117211

11

Single-Serve Control Premium?

Travis W. Harms, CFA, CPA/ABV
Originally Published on December 14, 2015

One of the perennial controversies in business valuation is the estimation of so-called control premiums. Following the closing of the comment period on the Appraisal Foundation's white paper on the topic,[1] control premiums were back in the news last week with announced acquisition of Keurig Green Mountain by JAB Holdings. The transaction's $92 per share purchase price rewarded investors with a 78% premium to the previous closing price. Compared to the often-cited range of benchmark control premiums between 30% and 40%, the JAB offer is an outlier. As such, what can we learn about control premiums by examining the proposed Keurig transaction a bit more closely?

Who is Keurig?

Keurig sells specialty coffee, coffeemakers, teas and other beverages in the United States and Canada. The Company's single-serve coffee makers are found on the countertops of over 20 million households, and the corresponding K-Cup coffee pods occupy significant shelf space in grocery and department stores. Historical financial results for Keurig are summarized in Figure 11.1.

Revenues grew rapidly during the early part of the decade as the Company's installed base of brewers expanded. Growth moderated in fiscal 2013 and 2014 before actually turning negative in 2015. The Company began paying a quarterly

Figure 11.1

		Fiscal Years Ended September			
	2011	2012	2013	2014	2015
Net Sales ($mil)	$2,650.9	$3,859.2	$4,358.1	$4,707.7	$4,520.0
Annual Growth Rate	*95.4%*	*45.6%*	*12.9%*	*8.0%*	*-4.0%*
Adjusted EBITDA	$509.0	$757.2	$999.3	$1,215.8	$1,078.5
Margin	*19.2%*	*19.6%*	*22.9%*	*25.8%*	*23.9%*

Source: Bloomberg, Mercer Capital analysis

Figure 11.2

		2015	2016	2017	2018	2019	Terminal
Revenue ($mil)		$4,520	$4,516	$4,655	$4,941	$5,089	
Annual Growth			*-0.1%*	*3.1%*	*6.1%*	*3.0%*	*3.0%*
EBITDA Margin		*23.9%*	*22.9%*	*23.2%*	*22.9%*	*23.0%*	
EBITDA		1,079	1,032	1,079	1,133	1,171	
less: Depr & Amort		266	255	265	296	300	
EBIT		813	777	814	837	871	
less: Pro Forma Taxes	35.0%		272	285	293	305	
Net Operating Profit After Tax			505	529	544	566	
plus: Depr & Amort			255	265	296	300	
less: Capital Expenditures			(255)	(265)	(296)	(300)	
less: Investment in Working Capital			1	(25)	(52)	(27)	
Cash Flow to Firm			506	504	492	539	9,018
Discounting Periods			0.5	1.5	2.5	3.5	3.5
Present Value Factors	9.2%		0.9572	0.8769	0.8034	0.7360	0.7360
Present Value of Cash Flows			484	442	395	396	6,637
Indicated Enterprise Value		$8,355					
EV / Fwd EBITDA		*8.1x*					

Source: Bloomberg, Mercer Capital analysis

dividend in January 2014. Introduced in 2015, Keurig's heralded cold-brew system for carbonated soft drinks was not well-received by the market.

Establishing a Baseline Set of Market Participant Expectations

The primary message of the Appraisal Foundation white paper is that buyers do not offer premiums simply for the sake of gaining control, but rather, because through exercising the prerogatives of control, those buyers expect to generate economic benefits (in the form of enhanced cash flows and growth, or a lower cost of capital). As a preliminary step to assessing the potential economic benefits available to a market participant for a controlling interest in a company, it is helpful to establish a baseline cash flow forecast and WACC that conforms to the pre-transaction, "foundation" value of the business.

The analysis in Figure 11.2 is based on market-consensus earnings estimates obtained from Bloomberg.

Prior to the transaction, Keurig's stock price represented an enterprise value of approximately $8.4 billion, or 8.1x forecast fiscal 2016 EBITDA. Given the market consensus earnings forecast through 2018 (and a series of generally benign assumptions regarding other cash flow items and long-term growth), the market price implied a WACC of approximately 9.2%.

Assessing Changes to Cash Flow, Risk, and Growth

The JAB Holdings offer corresponds to an enterprise value of approximately $14.5 billion, or 14.0x forward EBITDA. Using the analysis in Figure 11.1 as a base, we examined the implied adjustments to near-term revenue growth, EBITDA margin, and cost of capital that, individually, would generate an enterprise value equal to that implied by the JAB Holdings offer. Finally, we evaluated a composite set of changes to each factor that, in concert, generate a $14.5 billion enterprise value. The results of the analysis are summarized in Figure 11.3.

If there were no adjustments to market consensus expectations regarding EBITDA margin and cost of capital, JAB would need to anticipate incremental

Figure 11.3

	Baseline	Isolated Changes	Blended Changes
Interim (2016 - 2019) revenue growth	0% - 6%	20% - 26%	5% - 11%
EBITDA Margin	23%	35%	27%
Cost of Capital	9.2%	6.5%	8.2%
Enterprise Value	$8.4 billion	$14.5 billion	$14.5 billion

Source: Mercer Capital analysis

near-term revenue growth of 20% to justify the acquisition premium. Likewise, if revenue growth and cost of capital assumptions were unchanged, projected EBITDA margins would need to climb to 35% from the baseline level of 23%. While those isolated changes may strain credibility, the rightmost column summarizes the impact of smaller changes to each of the three primary value drivers. There are myriad combinations that would yield the same enterprise value; the noted adjustments represent a combination that is likely to be more representative of actual buyer expectations than any of the isolated adjustments identified in the middle column.

Market Participants

The analysis in Figure 11.3 reflects the terms of the JAB Holdings acquisition offer. Some background on JAB Holdings provides additional perspective on the offer. Acquirers are often identified as either "financial" (private equity) or "strategic" (competitors, customers, or suppliers). As described in a profile from *BloombergBusiness*, JAB seems to share traits of both acquirer types.[2] Owned by the Reimann family of Germany, JAB has invested in a number of consumer brand businesses, and began acquiring various global coffee assets in 2012, including Senseo, the coffee business of Mondelez, Caribou Coffee, and roaster/retailer Peet's [also premium "third-wave" micro-assets Stumptown and Intelligentsia]. Given this profile, the combination of incremental revenue growth, enhanced margins, and lower capital costs noted in Figure 11.2 makes sense. The profile linked above includes a quote from JAB's chairman Bart Becht summarizing the firm's recipe for investing success: "We bought consumer-goods businesses from companies for which it wasn't the primary interest. You could make a lot of changes and have a big impact." Translated into fair value idiom, they focus on expected changes to cash flow, risk, and growth. Acquisition premiums are outputs of their process, not inputs that determine what price to pay. JAB Capital is in many respects the platonic ideal of a market participant for controlling interests in businesses.

Premium in Context

Does the foregoing suggest that – in measuring fair value for reporting units – acquisition premiums on the order of 75% are always reasonable? Of course not. Just as Keurig's ubiquitous single-serve coffee pods are designed to deliver a tailored beverage experience, the facts and circumstances surrounding every fair value measurement will be unique. As Chart 11.1 illustrates, although the announced transaction price represented a substantial premium to the prior day's trading price, the transaction price represents a 65% discount to the Company's share price at the beginning of the year.

The stock price chart underscores the unique attributes of Keurig. While a declining stock price does not by itself support a large acquisition premium, a stock's trading history may provide some support for the overall reasonableness

Chart 11.1

of the inputs used to derive fair value from the perspective of a market participant acquiring control of a business. For Keurig, the decreasing stock price through 2015 had been a boon to short sellers, who learned that one motivated acquirer can quickly erase paper profits on short trades. In any event, the task of a fair value specialist is to thoroughly investigate the unique attributes of a subject business enterprise and carefully identify what factors may cause a market participant to pay an acquisition premium.

In the end, a fair value measurement is probably not all that different from a cup of coffee – the final product can only be as good as the inputs.

End Notes

[1] Exposure Draft - The Measurement and Application of Market Participant Acquisition Premiums. The Appraisal Foundation – Appraisal Practices Board. September 1, 2015. https://appraisalfoundation.sharefile.com/share#/view/s335af-45c4fe495d8/fi42541f-8295-a42c-73cc-7dbdbca19744

[2] de Jong, David and Matthew Boyle. "The Caffeine Fix." Bloomberg Markets. February 10, 2015. http://www.bloomberg.com/news/articles/2015-02-11/investor-trio-brews-coffee-deals-for-billionaire-siblings

Lands' End and Trade Name Impairment

Lucas Parris, CFA, ASA-BV/IA
Originally Published on February 1, 2016

Last week, Lands' End, Inc. (NASDAQ: LE) announced that it would write down the value of its flagship trade name asset (Lands' End). Management's preliminary guidance is for a charge of $90 million to $110 million, which could lower the asset's value by 20% from $528 million to $418 million. Obviously, a non-cash impairment charge is just that, non-cash, but what does it mean for stakeholders and how is such a charge actually determined?

Lands' End was purchased by Sears Holdings Corp. in 2002 for approximately $1.9 billion. Despite its plans to use Lands' End to bolster its online presence and attract more customers to its stores, Sears struggled to execute its strategy. The Company unsuccessfully attempted to sell the Lands' End business to a private equity buyer in 2012 and finally elected to spin off the business to existing shareholders as a separate publicly-traded company in April 2014.

As shown in Chart 17.1, total revenue has trended downward in recent years, including a decline of nearly 10% in the year-to-date period ended October 30, 2015. The company's fiscal year end follows a retail convention, ending on the Friday preceding the Saturday closest to January 31 each year. The decline in revenue was attributed to multiple factors, including a decrease in catalog circulation, lower customer acceptance in a challenging retail environment, and a decline in same-store walk-in sales. Adjusted EBITDA margin for the

Chart 17.1: Lands' End, Inc. Historical Summary

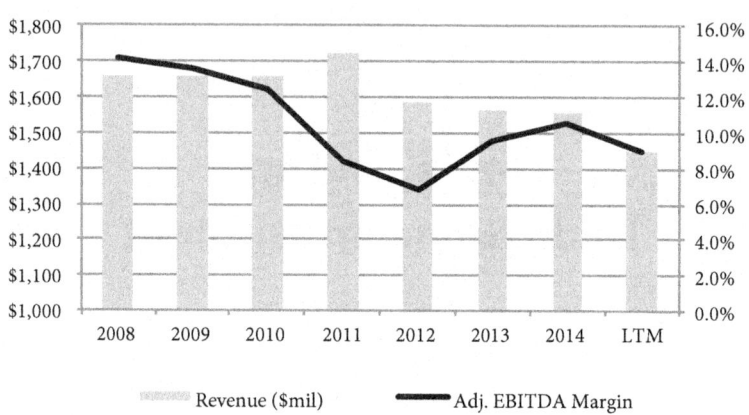

Source: Company filings through the 39 wks ended 10/30/2015 and Mercer Capital analysis. Adjusted EBITDA as defined by Company management.

company dipped from 10.6% of revenue in 2014 to 8.9% in the most recent twelve months.

In the SEC filing for the period ended October 30, 2015, management acknowledged that a continued decline in revenues could negatively impact future revenue forecasts and might lead to potential impairment charges.[1] It appears that this is exactly what happened.

The Lands' End trade name is classified as an indefinite-lived intangible asset with a carrying value of $528 million. The company's financial statements note that management uses the income approach, specifically the relief-from-royalty method, when testing the asset for potential impairment. The relief-from-royalty method seeks to measure the incremental net profitability generated by the owner of the subject intangible asset through the avoidance of royalty payments that would otherwise be required to enjoy the benefits of ownership of this asset. The primary inputs in the relief-from-royalty method are (1) the appropriate royalty rate to apply to the expected revenue stream, (2) the projected revenue stream itself, and (3) the appropriate discount rate used to measure the present value of the avoided royalty payments.

In the case of Lands' End, it is likely that the principal driver behind the impairment charge is a lower revenue forecast. Despite revenue fluctuations in the past, the company was not required to recognize an impairment charge in prior periods. In fact, the most recent 10-K filing noted that that fair value of the trade name exceeded its carrying value by 12%, which implies a fair value on the order of $591 million. At the current date, however, it may also be that the discount rate used to calculate the present value of the cash flows has increased. Through the end of January 2016, the company's stock price had declined by roughly 37% over the previous twelve months. Valuation is a function of cash flow, growth, and risk – and the risk part of that equation may have increased in light of a weakened competitive position.

What does such a charge portend for stakeholders? Academic studies frequently suggest that impairment charges (be they for goodwill or other intangible assets) are often already incorporated by investors into the stock price. Given the pressure on the Lands' End stock price over the last year, that may be the case here. One interesting note in this situation however, is that the trade name is the name and identity of the Company itself, not just the name of a product line or logo. In fact, the $528 million carrying value of the Lands' End name is nearly equal to the current equity market capitalization of the company (approximately $697 million as of the date of this writing) and almost half of the firm's total invested capital (including $502 million in interest bearing debt). It remains to be seen what charge the company will ultimately record and what steps management will take to turn the situation around.

End Note

[1] Available online: https://www.sec.gov/Archives/edgar/data/799288/00007992881 5000100/le2015103010q.htm

13

24-Hour Impairment: Merck's Drug Deal with Cubist

Samantha L. Albert
Originally Published on January 9, 2015

We wrote previously on *The Financial Reporting Blog* about an acquirer recording goodwill impairment charges only two months after an acquisition. While we remarked at the time that there is no defined period of time that must elapse before assets may be subject to impairment, the two month period was one of the shortest periods we had seen. Merck & Company (MRK) broke all land speed records, however, when the market effectively impaired the pharmaceutical giant for nearly the entirety of its pending purchase of Cubist Pharmaceuticals (CBST).

In a deal valued at approximately $9.5 billion ($8.4 million in cash and $1.1 in assumed debt), Merck's acquisition of Cubist was originally expected to result in significant EPS gains by 2016. At least, that was the plan. Mere hours after Merck's announcement, a U.S. court invalidated four of Cubist's five key patents on Cubicin, the antibiotic responsible for 80% of the company's revenue. The decision effectively allows generic production of Cubicin as early as June 2016, four and half years before the original patent expirations in November 2020.

The reaction in the markets was swift. When the market closed on December 8, 2014, before the court ruling was announced, Merck's stock price was $61.88 (equity market capitalization of $176.4 billion). The next day, Merck's stock opened at $59.40 (a 4.2% drop) and its market capitalization had been reduced by nearly $7.1 billion. Almost the entire value of the Cubist acquisition had been wiped out. Though the stock partially recovered to $60.11 by the end of that day, the effect on market capitalization was still a decline of over $5.0 billion. For its part, Merck claims that the court's decision, which is subject to appeal, does not change the company's expectations for the transaction and that the acquisition of Cubist will still create strong fundamental value for shareholders.

So did investors overreact? Perhaps. In the month since the announcement, Merck's shares have risen nearly 2.0%, but it is difficult to tell whether this is due to calmer heads, fundamentals, or other market factors. The FDA did approve another of Cubist's drugs, Zerbaxa, on December 19th. In any event, the court's decision on Cubicin will almost certainly factor into the company's assessment of goodwill arising from the deal, if it is indeed consummated. Some analysts have noted that it is unlikely that Merck could back out of the deal because a negative legal outcome is not counted as a "material adverse event" in the merger agreement. Cubist's stock price seems to bear that out, as it has remained just shy of the merger consideration price ($102.00/share) since late December.

14

Goodwill Impairment: Good, Bad, or Indifferent?

Lucas Parris, CFA, ASA-BV/IA
Originally Published on July 2, 2014

A recent article from McKinsey & Company examined investor reaction to news of a goodwill impairment.[1] Through analysis of excess returns in the three days before and after announcement, McKinsey found that investors often respond positively, or neutrally, when companies announce a goodwill write-down. Why wouldn't investors react more negatively? The authors suggest that when investors already understand that an acquisition has been underperforming, the impairment charge may be perceived as an event that communicates acknowledgment on the part of management as well as an opportunity to change course.

The article goes on to encourage companies to be candid with investors about the nature of the impairment and the company's plans to address the situation and move forward. Further, the article suggests that "[e]xecutives should also record as much of the impairment or restructuring charges as possible in a single announcement" as a lot of bad news at one time may be easier for investors to digest (and forgive) than a dribble of bad news over a longer period of time.

While we understand the practical reasoning behind the notion of taking all of your medicine at one time, we believe the amount of impairment should be consistent with the facts and circumstances (including market participant assumptions) extant at the measurement date – no less, no more. The logic and mechanics of testing goodwill for impairment might still be debated in some circles, but the accounting and compliance requirements have firmed up in recent years. For evidence of this, look no further than the recent updates to ASC Topic 350 – Intangibles – Goodwill and Other as well as the AICPA's recently published *Accounting and Valuation Guide, Testing Goodwill for Impairment.*

At the end of the day, the McKinsey findings are generally consistent with what we observe as we assist companies with the goodwill impairment testing process. We're heartened to now have additional evidence that, by-and-large, the public markets tend to have a mature reaction to news of goodwill impairment.

End Note

[1]   Cao, Bing, Marc Goedhart, and Tim Koller. "Goodwill shunting: How to better manager write-downs." McKinsey & Company. June 2014. http://www.mckinsey.com/business-functions/strategy-and-corporate-finance/our-insights/goodwill-shunting-how-to-better-manage-write-downs

15

Pulling the Trigger: Interim Goodwill Impairment Testing

Originally Published on March 14, 2016

Most financial professionals understand that goodwill impairment testing is typically performed annually. However, ASC 350 also prescribes that interim goodwill tests may be necessary in the case of certain "triggering" events. For public companies, perhaps the most common triggering event is a decline in stock price, but a variety of other factors may constitute a triggering event as described in ASC 350 including the following:

- Changes in the macroeconomic environment, including fluctuations in exchanges rates and the tightening of credit markets

- Changes within the relevant industry or industries such as decreases in market multiples

- Cost factor considerations

- Poor financial performance, negative cash flows, significant short falls from budgeted or projected performance

- Entity-specific events (changes in management, adverse litigation or regulatory events)

- Changes in the carrying amount of assets at the reporting unit including the expectation of selling or disposing certain assets

- Sustained decreases in share price (if applicable)

The list is far from exhaustive or definitive. For example, more nuanced triggering events might include circumstances such as the inability to effectively enforce a non-compete agreement. Additionally, not all events described in ASC 350 may qualify as triggering events in certain circumstances. Market capitalization may cease to be a reliable indicator in times of high volatility, particularly for companies with more than one reporting unit.

For example, as Blockbuster Inc. grappled with changes in the entertainment industry, the company performed an interim impairment test in the third quarter of 2005, citing the following factors as triggering events:

> *"(i) increased competition from retail mass merchant sales of low-priced DVDs, online rentals and other sources of in-home entertainment such as digital video recorders and other devices that are capable of downloading content for in-home viewing; (ii) competition from piracy in certain international markets; and (iii) competition from other forms of leisure entertainment."* [1]

As a result of the interim impairment test, Blockbuster recognized a goodwill impairment charge of $332 million in its international reporting unit. However, the interim test did not result in any impairment charges related to domestic reporting unit.

While Blockbuster ultimately filed for bankruptcy in 2010, it is important to emphasize that a triggering event by itself does not necessarily imply impairment, as demonstrated by the 2005 test for the domestic unit. The trigger merely indicates that goodwill needs to be reviewed through either a Step 0 or a Step 1 Test. It may well be that the fair value of a reporting unit still exceeds its carrying value, implying no impairment.

For reporting units undergoing major changes, interim goodwill impairment testing provides management, auditors, and investors with some assurance that the unit's balance sheet reflects the current expectations for the unit.

End Note

[1]   Form 10-K for the year ended December 31, 2005.

16

Free to a Good Home: Assigning Balance Sheet Items to Reorganized Reporting Units

Originally Published on November 1, 2013

One of the challenges faced by companies in the goodwill impairment testing process involves estimating the carrying value of a reporting unit when the corporate structure of the business has been reorganized. ASC 350-20-35-39 provides guidance on assigning acquired assets and assumed liabilities to a reporting unit for goodwill impairment testing. In the ideal scenario, this process takes place during the initial purchase price allocation for an acquisition or merger. Tangible and intangible assets as well as the associated liabilities are measured at fair value and allocated to relevant reporting units.

Businesses are dynamic though, and as a company changes its products, services, and geographic markets, the need for new reporting units may emerge. Resources are often shared between reporting units. How should a firm go about determining which of these existing balance sheet items are allocated to the new reporting units? According to ASC 350, assigned balance sheet items should (1) relate to the operations of the reporting unit, and (2) be considered in the determination of the fair value of the reporting unit.

ASC 350-20-35-40 states:

> "The methodology used to determine the amount of those assets or liabilities to assign to a reporting unit shall be reasonable and supportable and shall be applied in a consistent manner."

The general nature of this guidance results in a number of possible methods that may be used to allocate balance sheet items between reporting units. Items may be allocated of the basis of relative sales, the number of employees, or on the basis of underlying business economics and capital needs. Certain items may require additional analysis in determining what value is appropriate to assign to each reporting unit. The equity allocated to each reporting unit may be tested for reasonableness by performing a valuation of each reporting unit. Likewise, items such as goodwill and intangible assets may require further analysis to determine the appropriate reporting unit assignment.

As businesses evolve, so do their financial reporting needs. Proper assignment of balance sheet items to reporting units can help ensure a smoother goodwill impairment testing process going forward.

Purchase Price
Allocations &
Intangibles

17

Yes, Virginia, the Cost of Capital Really Is Low

Travis W. Harms, CFA, CPA/ABV
Originally Published on August 14, 2015

When Berkshire Hathaway (BRK) announced the planned acquisition of Precision Castparts (PCP), pundits described the $37 billion purchase price as "hefty".[1] Has Mr. Buffett forsaken his legendary investment discipline, or does the hefty price tag highlight one consequence of the Fed's persistent zero-interest rate policy (ZIRP)?

The heft of any particular purchase price can really only be evaluated relative to the (expected) earnings stream acquired. For public market investors, the ratio of stock price to earnings per share is the most commonly cited relative pricing measure. When entire operating companies are transacted, the common measure of relative value is that of enterprise value to earnings before interest, taxes, depreciation and amortization or EBITDA. Enterprise value, the sum of equity and net debt, represents the value of the total company, regardless of how it is financed. Similarly, EBITDA is a broad measure of earnings that is unaffected by a company's capital structure and common non-cash charges.

Comparing the reported transaction value ($37.2 billion) to the consensus estimate for forward EBITDA ($3.0 billion) yields an EV/EBITDA ratio of 12.3x. By way of comparison, Thomson Reuters reports that the average EBITDA multiple for leveraged buyouts in the broadly syndicated market (i.e., large deals) through the first seven months of 2015 was 10.2x. After peaking at 10.8x in 2008, average EBITDA multiples fell to 9.1x in 2009 and have gradually increased to

Chart 12.1: Precision Castparts Corp.

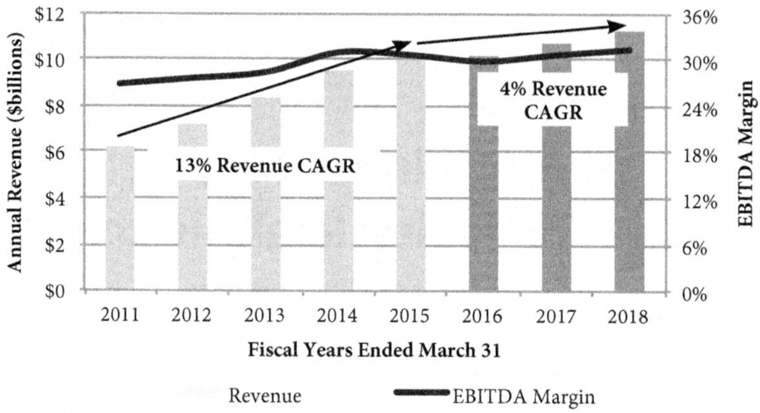

Fiscal Years Ended March 31

Revenue ———EBITDA Margin

Source: Consensus analyst estimates (FY 16 – FY18) from Bloomberg L.P.; Mercer Capital

current levels since then. So, relative to the average multiple, the EBITDA multiple of 12.3x paid for Precision Castparts is high.

While more informative than absolute price, an EBITDA multiple still fails to communicate the prospective return anticipated by investors. If a forecast of future earnings and cash flows is available, one can derive the prospective return on a transaction. As a hitherto publicly-traded company, consensus analyst estimates are available for PCP.

Historical revenue growth as shown in Chart 12.1 was buttressed by a series of acquisitions representing an aggregate investment of over $8 billion. The forecast results do not contemplate additional acquisitions, so the projected revenue growth of approximately 4% corresponds to an organic growth rate. Augmented by a small amount of margin expansion, the growth rate in projected EBITDA is 5%. Projected cash flows are derived by deducting taxes and net investment in fixed assets and working capital from EBITDA, as shown in Figure 12.1.

Comparing the projected cash flows to the purchase price yields an internal rate of return of 8.2%. This is the unlevered return on the aggregate purchase price. From the perspective of Berkshire Hathaway shareholders, the use of debt financing increases the prospective equity returns. Berkshire is reportedly financing the purchase using $23 billion of cash reserves and borrowing the balance.

Figure 12.1: Precision Castparts Corp.

		Fiscal Years Ended March 31,				
	2015	2016	2017	2018	2019	Terminal
Revenue	$10,005	$10,167	$10,718	$11,273	$11,724	
Annual Growth		*1.6%*	*5.4%*	*5.2%*	***4.0%***	*3.0%*
EBITDA Margin	*29.3%*	*29.8%*	*30.7%*	*31.3%*	***31.5%***	
EBITDA	2,929	3,030	3,287	3,533	3,693	
less: Depr & Amort	325	302	330	344	350	
EBIT	2,604	2,728	2,957	3,189	3,343	
less: Pro Forma Taxes	32.1%		877	950	1,025	1,074
Net Operating Profit After Tax		1,851	2,007	2,164	2,269	
plus: Depr & Amort		302	330	344	350	
less: Capital Expenditures		(514)	(444)	(448)	(400)	
less: Investment in Working Capital		(61)	(207)	(209)	(170)	
Cash Flow to Firm		1,579	1,685	1,852	2,049	40,927
Discounting Periods		0.5	1.5	2.5	3.5	3.5
Present Value Factors	8.2%	0.9616	0.8890	0.8220	0.7600	0.7600
Present Value of Cash Flows		1,518	1,498	1,522	1,557	31,105
Indicated Enterprise Value	**$37,200**					
EV / Fwd EBITDA	*12.3x*					

Source: Consensus analyst estimates (FY16-FY18) from Bloomberg, LP; Mercer Capital analysis

Figure 12.2

	$Billions	% of Total	Multiple of Fwd EBITDA
Source of Funds			
Debt	$14.2	38.2%	4.7x
Equity	23.0	61.8%	7.6x
Total Purchase Price	$37.2	100.0%	12.3x

Figure 12.3

	% of Total	Capital Costs
Source of Funds		
Debt	38.2%	4.2%
Equity	**61.8%**	**10.6%**
Total Purchase Price	100.0%	8.2%

The implied debt in the pro forma capital structure equals approximately 4.7x EBITDA, compared to total leverage of 6.1x for large corporate LBOs in 2015 (per Thomson Reuters). From that perspective, the financing mix is conservative. Although the cost of the acquisition debt has not been disclosed, Thomson Reuters reports that the average first-lien institutional spread on large corporate leveraged loans during 3Q15 has been 388 basis points. Using this average rate as a proxy, the after-tax cost of debt (on a fixed-equivalent basis) is approximately 4.2%, implying a levered equity return of 10.6%.

So the "hefty" price implies a return for equity investors in excess of 10%. As with absolute price, absolute return is less meaningful than relative return. Comparing the prospective equity return of 10.6% to the return on long-term treasuries (approximately 2.5%), the implied equity risk premium is in excess of 8%. By way of comparison, most estimates of the market-wide equity risk premium are in the range of 4% to 7%.

Because of the wide availability of low-cost debt, even a "hefty" purchase multiple does not necessarily obliterate prospective equity returns. Berkshire Hathaway's purchase of Precision Castparts provides a timely illustration of the practical effect of the Fed's accommodative monetary policy on corporate costs of capital and valuation multiples.

End Note

[1] Stempel, Jonathan, Sagarika Jaisinghani, and Sweta Singh. "Buffet pays high price for Precision Castparts." Reuters. August 10, 2015. http://www.reuters.com/article/us-precision-cast-m-a-berkshire-hatha-idUSKCN0QD0LD20150810

18

Valuation of Customer-Related Assets

Lucas Parris, CFA, ASA-BV/IA and Sujan Rajbhandary, CFA
Originally Published on January 11, 2016

Customer relationships form a key intangible asset for firms operating in many industries. Firms devote significant human and financial resources in developing, maintaining and upgrading customer relationships. In some instances, supply or customer contracts give rise to identifiable intangible assets. More broadly, however, customer related intangible assets consist of the information gleaned from repeat transactions, with or without underlying contracts. Firms can and do lease, sell, buy or otherwise trade such information, which are generally organized as customer lists.

The Appraisal Practices Board of The Appraisal Foundation originally released a discussion draft of a document entitled "The Valuation of Customer-Related Assets" in June 2012. The draft, authored by the Working Group on Customer-Related Assets, provides best practices guidance on the valuation of customer-related intangible assets. A subsequent exposure draft was released in December 2013. A final version of the document is pending. This article, drawing in part from these documents, examines attributes of customer-related intangible assets and their valuation.

Value Attributes

Three key attributes are important in considering the value of customer-related intangible assets:

1. The expectation of repeat patronage creates value for customer-related intangible assets. Contractual customer relationships formally codify the expectation of future transactions. Even in the absence of contracts, firms look to build on past interactions with customers to sell products and services in the future. Two aspects of repeat patronage are important in evaluating customer relationships. First, not all customer contact leads to an expectation of repeat patronage. The quality of interaction with walk-up retail customers, for instance, is generally considered inadequate to reliably lead to expectations of recurring business. Second, even in the presence of adequate information, not all expected repeat business may be attributable to customer-related intangible assets. Some firms operate in monopolistic or near-monopolistic industries where repeat patronage is directly attributable to a lack of acceptable alternatives available to customers. In other cases, it may be more appropriate to attribute recurring business to the strength of the trade names or brands.

2. Customer-related intangible assets create value over a finite period. Without efforts geared towards continual reinforcement, customer lists dwindle over time due to customer mortality, the ravages of competition, or the emergence of alternate products and services. The mechanics of present value mathematics further erode the economic benefits of sales to current customers in the distant future. Customer relationships are wasting assets whose economic value deteriorates with the passage of time.

3. Customer-related intangible assets depend on the existence of other assets to provide value to the firm. Most assets, including fixed assets and intellectual property, are essential in creating products or providing services. The act of selling these products and services enable firms to develop relationships and collect information from customers. In turn, the value of these relationships depends on the firms' ability to sell additional products and services in the future. Consequently, for firms to extract value from customer related assets, a number of other assets need to be in place.

Why Value Customer-Related Assets?

The need for the valuation of customer-related intangible assets for financial reporting purposes may arise in primarily two contexts:

- **Acquisition accounting**. Following business or asset acquisitions, ASC 805 Business Combinations requires firms to recognize and measure the fair value of acquired identifiable assets, including any customer-related intangible asset. Certain exceptions for private companies may be available.

- **Impairment testing**. ASC 350 *Intangibles – Goodwill and Other* currently mandates a multi-step goodwill impairment test to be conducted (at least) annually. Under Step 1, firms measure the fair value of the reporting units being tested. If the carrying amount of a reporting unit exceeds its fair value, Step 2 of the test is triggered. Step 2 requires firms to measure the fair value of all identifiable assets, including any customer-related intangible asset, of the reporting units. However, the FASB is considering the elimination of the Step 2 requirement.

Additionally, ASC 360 *Property, Plant, and Equipment* sets forth the procedures for impairment testing of long-lived assets (including any customer-related intangible asset) held and used, or assets held for sale or disposal.

Fair value, for the purposes of both acquisition accounting and impairment testing, is defined in ASC 820 Fair Value Measurement as "the price that would be received to sell an asset or paid to transfer a liability in an orderly transaction between market participants at the measurement date."

In particular, fair value is defined from the perspective of market participants rather than a specific party. Accordingly, valuation of customer-related intangible assets should be based on market participant assumptions.

Valuation Methodologies

Valuation methods generally fall into one of three approaches: cost, market or income.

- Valuation under the cost approach requires estimation of the cost to replace the subject asset, as well as opportunity costs in the form of cash flows foregone as the replacement is sought or recreated. The cost approach may not be feasible when replacement or recreation periods are long. Therefore, the cost approach is used infrequently in valuing customer-related assets.

- Use of the market approach in valuing customer-related assets is generally untenable because transactional data on sufficiently comparable assets are not likely to be available.

- Under the income approach, fair value estimates are based on cash flows that an asset is expected to generate in the future. In practice, customer-related assets are valued most commonly using the multi period excess earnings method (MPEEM) under the income approach. Other techniques include the distributor method, the with-and-without method, and the differential cash flows method.

Applying the Multi-Period Excess Earnings Method

MPEEM involves estimation of the cash flow stream attributable to a particular asset. The cash flow stream is discounted to the present to obtain an indication of fair value. The most common starting point in estimating future cash flows is the prospective financial information prepared by (or in close consultation with) the management of the subject business.

In applying the MPEEM to customer-related assets, valuation professionals first identify the portion of prospective revenues that is expected to be generated through repeat business from customers existing at the valuation date. It is often useful to examine estimated future revenue as the product of revenue per customer and the number of retained customers. Fair value measurement requires that valuation professionals consider prospective revenue from a market participant perspective and exclude any firm-specific synergies that may be embedded in the prospective financial information prepared by management.

As discussed earlier, customer-related assets derive value within a finite period as the numbers of customers that provide repeat business can be expected to decline over time. Good estimates of expected attrition can be obtained by conducting statistical analyses of historical customer turnover and revenue growth rates. When historical customer data of sufficient quality is not available, it may be necessary to rely on management estimates or an examination of industry characteristics in developing customer attrition rates.

After the identification of prospective revenues attributable to the base of customers existing at the valuation date, valuation professionals estimate earnings based on expected profitability of the business. It is important to consider only the operating costs relevant to the base of existing customers from a market participant perspective. Marketing costs that are expected to be necessary in finding new customers and firm specific cost synergies, for instance, are not relevant in projecting earnings on expected revenue from existing customers.

Cash flow attributable to the customer-related asset is isolated from the estimated earnings by assessing contributory charges for other assets of the subject business. As discussed earlier, a number of other assets need to be in place for firms to extract value from customer related assets. The contributory charges represent economic rent equivalent to returns on and returns of assets necessary to produce goods or services marketed to the customers.

19

Valuation of Contingent Consideration in M&A Transactions

Lucas Parris, CFA, ASA-BV/IA
Originally Published on March 14, 2016

Companies often use contingent consideration when structuring M&A transactions to bridge differing perceptions of value between a buyer and seller, to share risk related to uncertainty of future events, to create an incentive for sellers who will remain active in the business post-acquisition, and other reasons. ASC 805 stipulates that acquiring entities are required to record the fair value of earnouts and other contingent payments as part of the total purchase price at the acquisition date.

The Rules

ASC 805, the section of the FASB codification that addresses business combinations, requires that:

- The fair value of contingent consideration be recognized and measured at fair value at the acquisition date. In most cases, recognition of a liability for contingent consideration will increase the amount of goodwill recognized in the transaction.

- Fair value must be re-measured for each subsequent reporting date until resolution of the contingency, and any increases or decreases in fair value will show up on the income statement as an operating loss or gain.

What Is Fair Value?

In the case of contingent consideration, fair value represents the amount the reporting entity would have to pay a hypothetical counter-party to transfer responsibility for paying the contingent liability. This amount is basically the present value of the probability-weighted expected amount of the future payment.

Valuation Procedures

The complexity of the procedures necessary to estimate the future payment ultimately depends on the structure of the earn-out.

- For an earn-out structured as a straight multiple of revenue or EBITDA, it may be reasonable in many cases to estimate the expected payment using a single-scenario model by applying that multiple directly to the measure of performance in the financial forecast.

- For a fixed amount payable upon achieving a particular milestone or event, estimating probabilities of various scenarios in a multi-scenario model will be necessary.

- For more complicated earn-outs including thresholds, caps, or tiers, a more complicated modeling technique such as a Monte Carlo simulation or real options analysis will be required. Preparing these analyses generally requires specialized training and software.

Valuation Inputs

For earn-out structures including milestone payments or tiered schedules, the fair value of the contingent payment is generally most sensitive to the estimate of the probability-weighted expected payment (rather than other inputs such as duration of contingency or discount rate). Developing reasonable estimates of the probability of future events is inherently difficult, but the use of ***decomposition*** and cross-checks will help improve the quality of these estimates. Decomposition is the process of breaking down a big event (such as commercialization of a development-stage product) into a series of smaller, more familiar pieces to make the probability estimate process easier. *Cross-checks* using aggregate industry information (such as the average length of time to receive regulatory approval from the FDA) can be helpful to validate assumptions that by nature rely on judgment. Industry expertise can be extremely valuable when selecting a valuation specialist to help with estimating the fair value of contingent consideration. An expert will be able to decompose common pathways into a series of manageable steps to estimate, will have familiarity with available industry data that can be used to help support assumptions, and will be able to effectively explain and defend the assumptions.

Role of a Valuation Specialist

In most cases, you or someone else in your company will likely be the individual most knowledgeable of the potential outcomes. The role of the valuation specialist is to integrate this information into the appropriate valuation model, test it for reasonableness, and to articulate the nuances of the inputs and valuation model in such a way that is clear for auditors and other third-party reviewers to understand. For simple situations it may not be necessary to bring in the outside help of a valuation specialist. For more complicated situations requiring multiple scenarios or Monte Carlo analysis, however, outside support may be necessary. If you have any questions regarding the valuation of contingent consideration or the impact of particular structures on financial reporting procedures, feel free to contact us in confidence.

20

Economics of Elon Musk's Patent Altruism

Originally Published on June 20, 2014

Elon Musk just opened Tesla Motors' patents to the public in "the spirit of the open source movement" (and maybe as a subtle dig at its namesake's biggest rival, Thomas Edison).[1,2] Mr. Musk is a cofounder of Zip2 and PayPal; founder, CEO, and chief designer of SpaceX; cofounder, CEO, and product architect of Tesla Motors; and Chairman of SolarCity. He has bet, with the help of his companies' innovations, that solar power will provide a plurality of our energy in less than 20 years and that humanity will step foot on Mars in 10 to 12 years.[3] He often makes some iteration of the following self-deprecating joke:

> *"Did you hear the one about the guy who made a small fortune in the space industry? He started with a large one."*

With the various successes of Tesla Motors, SpaceX, and SolarCity in the last year, the market seems to think otherwise. In an ostensibly altruistic act, Mr. Musk stated last week that "Tesla will not initiate patent lawsuits against anyone who, in good faith, wants to use our technology." So, what are these patents that Tesla Motor's cofounder is seemingly giving away actually worth?

Most important to a patent's value is its ability to enhance cash flows by either direct monetization (royalties) or higher margins from lower competition. Conceptually, it's best to use some combination of the following approaches:

- **Cost approach**: how much it would cost to recreate the patent;

- **Market approach**: the price at which market participants would agree to transact the patent; and,

- **Income approach**: future cash flows (likely amounts and associated variability) attributable to the patent.

Further, the ability of a patent to enhance cash flows is inextricably linked to the enforceability of the exclusive right to a product or process that it provides. If a court will not uphold the patent, then it is worthless as it provides no revenue or competitive advantage. Mr. Musk has been a skeptic of patents for years. In regard to lack of SpaceX patents on their spacecraft and rockets, he stated in a TED interview over a year ago, "Since our biggest competition is national governments, the enforceability of patents is questionable." [4]

He wrote in his recent press release, "a patent really just meant that you bought a lottery ticket to a lawsuit, I avoided them whenever possible." Mr. Musk went on to say:

> "At Tesla, however, we felt compelled to create patents out of concern that the big car companies would copy our technology and then use their massive manufacturing, sales and marketing power to overwhelm Tesla. We couldn't have been more wrong. The unfortunate reality is the opposite: electric car programs (or programs for any vehicle that doesn't burn hydrocarbons) at the major manufacturers are small to non-existent, constituting an average of far less than 1% of their total vehicle sales."

If no one's using the technology, and there are no royalties, are the patents worthless? Has Mr. Musk found himself with the only fax machine on the planet? While a great invention, the value of faxing was only partly in the plastic box—most of the technology's value can be attributed to a robust and near-ubiquitous network of machines that made wide-scale document transmission feasible.

An electric car, without a cost-effective nationwide network of charging infrastructure, is likely a novelty without much use outside of short, daily commutes. By giving away these patents, Mr. Musk probably hopes to create a system of sufficient size to overcome the cost of his nationwide recharging stations—not just the cost of building the stations, but waiting times or just the psychological signal that buying and waiting for electric vehicles to charge is acceptable behavior. We have actually seen similar moves with emerging technologies before: Bessemer steel mills and General Motors' catalytic converters are just two examples. [5, 6]

During a conference call on his recent decision, he stated, "You want to be innovating so fast that you invalidate your prior patents, in terms of what really matters. It's the velocity of innovation that matters." Elon Musk is likely investing in future demand for his next generation of patents. Ultimately, one has to assume that Mr. Musk is trying to drum up demand for his wares: Tesla's third generation Model X, batteries from its new factory, or solar power built and financed by SolarCity. Perhaps shrewdly, he appears to have concluded that the cash flows he is giving up today in the form of foregone royalties or potentially lower margins will be more than made up by future cash flows from a more vibrant solar power-based transportation network.

End Notes

[1]   "All Our Patent Are Belong To You," https://www.tesla.com/blog/all-our-patent-are-belong-you

[2]   "Thomas Edison was a Patent Troll," http://www.slate.com/articles/technology/history_of_innovation/2014/05/thomas_edison_charles_goodyear_and_elias_howe_jr_were_patent_trolls.html

[3]   "Elon Musk: Just Watch Me – I'll Put Human Boots on Mars by 2026," http://www.theregister.co.uk/2014/06/18/spacex_can_get_mankind_on_mars_in_10_or_12_years_claims_elon_musk/

[4]   "The Mind Behind Tesla, SpaceX, SolarCity..." http://www.ted.com/talks/elon_musk_the_mind_behind_tesla_spacex_solarcity

[5]   "History Backs Up Tesla's Patent Sharing," https://hbr.org/2014/06/history-backs-up-teslas-patent-sharing?utm_content=buffer559e5&utm_medium=social&utm_source=twitter.com&utm_campaign=buffer%20via%20@HarvardBiz

[6]   "Tesla's Apparent Altruism with its Patents is Just Smart Business," http://www.scmp.com/business/companies/article/1535402/teslas-apparent-altruism-its-patents-just-smart-business

21

What's Up with WhatsApp?

Samantha L. Albert and Lucas Parris, CFA, ASA-BV/IA
Originally Published on March 6, 2015

About a year ago, Facebook purchased the messaging service WhatsApp. At the time, the acquisition was the subject of much debate, but the intervening period gives us a chance to see how things have shaken out. This also shows how the purchase price has been allocated for accounting purposes.

Facebook's allocation of WhatsApp's intangible assets is shown below, along with the purchase price allocations from several similar transactions.

Facebook allocated $2.0 billion (11% of total assets) to "acquired users." At the transaction's announcement date, WhatsApp had a user base in excess of 450 million people worldwide.[1] WhatsApp's users are not contractually bound to the company and the service costs just $0.99 per year after one year of free use. The rough math on that would suggest potential revenue of approximately $445 million annually from acquired users. The useful life ascribed to the "acquired users" asset is seven years.

Now that the user base has surpassed 700 million, the potential for revenue has likewise increased.[2] However, WhatsApp's recent revenue numbers do not bestow the potential maximum. In fiscal 2013, WhatsApp generated $10.2 million in revenue and posted a net loss in excess of $138 million. For fiscal 2014, WhatsApp revenue was just $21 million, as implied by pro forma disclosure in Facebook's most recent Form 10-K. Facebook's recognition of such a substantial allocation of purchase price to the user base presumably reflected the expectation of potentially enormous profit from the acquired users. Additionally, the WhatsApp user base metadata could also be independently valuable to Facebook. Although WhatsApp has not traditionally sold ads, such data could allow Facebook to refine its own processes.

In general, it appears that the goodwill allocation resulting from the acquisition is typical of similar tech/messaging transactions. Compared to the sample of deals shown above, WhatsApp's allocation of 85% is greater than all but YouTube's 87%. Allocations to tradename and technology (including both in-process and developed technology) are generally in line with the comparable transactions.

Figure 21.1

As a % of Total Assets Acquired	Facebook / WhatsApp 10/6/14	Facebook / Instagram 9/6/12	Yahoo / Tumblr 6/19/13	Microsoft / Yammer 7/18/12	Microsoft / Skype 10/13/11	Google / YouTube 11/13/06
Tangible Assets	0%	0%	8%	0%	0%	0%
Technology	2%	13%	2%	6%	3%	2%
Tradenames	3%	11%	5%	3%	14%	12%
Customer-Related	0%	0%	17%	7%	1%	0%
Acquired Users	11%	0%	0%	0%	0%	0%
Goodwill	85%	76%	68%	84%	81%	87%
Total Goodwill ($mil)	$15,342	$433	$751	$937	$7,100	$1,135
Trans. Value ($mil)	$17,193	$521	$990	$1,115	$8,526	$1,194
Goodwill / Trans. Value	89%	83%	76%	84%	83%	95%

Source: Company filings, Mercer Capital analysis

How does Facebook explain the 85% allocation to goodwill? Per the Company's 2014 Form 10-K, goodwill from the WhatsApp acquisition was attributable to "expected synergies from future growth, from potential monetization opportunities, from strategic advantages provided in the mobile ecosystem, and from expansion of our mobile messaging offerings." It remains to be seen whether these synergies will truly translate into measurable value and cash flow.

End Notes

[1] Available online:https://www.sec.gov/Archives/edgar/data/1326801/000132680114000010/exhibit991_pressrelease219.htm

[2] Available online: http://readwrite.com/2015/01/06/whatsapp-700-million/

22

Get with the Times:
The Fair Value of "Big Data"

Sujan Rajbhandary, CFA
Originally Published on October 17, 2014

Consider the following eclectic assortment of vignettes:

- A few weeks ago, some colleagues from Mercer Capital attended the demo day for a Memphis-based summer startup accelerator. One of the presenting companies was developing a platform to match consumers who want to swap excess make-up supplies. Interestingly, the founder's vision for creating value was based on more than the utility created for swappers. The second-side of the business would harvest, process, analyze, and package swap data to be sold to make-up buying clubs, manufacturers and marketers.

- "Data scientist," a job title or description that was almost non-existent just a few years ago has now become a very important function within young startups across all segments, as well as traditional firms like retailers and banks.[1] Data scientists with two years of experience can earn upwards of $200,000 a year, which is presumably reflective of the high demand for these positions.

- As a consumer, I have received "bespoke" (customized) coupons from Kroger that are based, presumably, on my purchase history with the grocery store. Some of the coupons are astonishingly relevant – they seem to know when I need to buy the next set of razor-blades – but most miss the mark, sometimes hilariously so. If I were a gambling man, however, I would not wager against these coupons becoming more and more useful to the point of being indispensable in the future, especially if Kroger decides to procure data on my interactions outside the four walls of their stores and incorporate them into their coupon-generating algorithms.

A recent WSJ article indicates that transaction-crossing platforms like traditional brick-and-mortar stores or online markets can and do collect data that consumer-product manufacturers are willing to purchase in order to fine-tune their own products and marketing.[2] For instance, the article estimates that Kroger's revenue from selling this type of data is on the order of $100 million annually. It would be logical to assume that the process of generating some, if not all, of the bespoke coupons mailed by Kroger is influenced by the fine-tuned marketing efforts on the part of the manufacturers.

Beyond traditional businesses, big data underpins the business models of tech companies – ranging from giants like Google and Facebook, to months-old startups – that collect information from their users on the one hand, and use that data to provide tailored advertising (or other) solutions on the other. At the moment, however, users of financial statements are unlikely to find assets that correspond to these datasets (and the resources invested in processing them) on the balance sheets of many companies, as the WSJ article notes:

> *Kroger does say that it follows generally accepted accounting principles, which prohibit companies from treating data as an asset or counting money spent collecting and analyzing the data as investments instead of costs.*

Current accounting treatment stipulates that in-process research and development efforts are expensed as costs but capitalized as assets following business combinations (mergers and acquisitions). The WSJ article suggests that measuring the fair value of a "big data" asset may be difficult because "companies also would have to estimate the shelf-life of their data, figure out its future worth and track and report any changes in its value." For fair value practitioners, however, these concerns may not seem insurmountable. Indeed, much like customer-related intangible assets, the following elements are likely key in reasonably considering the fair value of big data intangible assets:

- Revenue generated through the sales of the datasets can be a direct input in measuring fair value.

- In the absence of direct data sales, the expectation of enhanced product sales – by increasing customer retention, identifying better product fit, developing methods to maximize sales prices (through differential pricing, for example), or otherwise – can support the value of these assets.

- Historical or projected replacement cycles can be illustrative in determining the period over which these assets lose their ability to enhance product sales.

- As firms would need to assemble a number of other assets for the datasets to be valuable, a mechanism to consider contributory asset charges could also be necessary.

At the end of the day, financial statements need to reflect current economic realities to stay relevant. Tangible physical assets may have been the primary source of value creation in an earlier era, but intangible assets increasingly drive the business models of a newer generation of firms. While a degree of judgment is necessary in measuring their fair value, perhaps it is time to reconsider the need to recognize certain intangible assets on the balance sheets of companies even in the absence of (or prior to) business combinations.

End Notes

[1]   "Big Data's High Priests of Algorithms," http://www.wsj.com/articles/academic-researchers-find-lucrative-work-as-big-data-scientists-1407543088

[2]   "The Big Mystery: What's Big Data Really Worth?" http://www.wsj.com/articles/whats-all-that-data-worth-1413157156

23

Secrets of the Tech Road: The Evolving Status of Non-Competes

Originally Published on May 2, 2014

For hundreds of years, various Chinese dynasties prevented the dissemination of their sericultural secrets along the Silk Road by punishment of death. If anyone were caught smuggling a silkworm egg or cocoon or revealing any information about silk production, well, it would be off with their head. While axes have fallen out of fashion as the weapon of choice for protecting intellectual property, some might argue that they have been replaced by the equally controversial non-compete agreements (NCAs).

In an attempt to promote innovation in technology industries, Massachusetts is considering the adoption of policies to all but eliminate employee non-compete agreements (certain sales of a business are one exception), modeled after California legislation where courts have essentially refused to enforce them.[1] The business sale exception would permit non-compete agreements when the restricted party owns at least 10% of the business. Massachusetts is also considering adoption of The Uniform Trade Secrets Act as part of the same bill, which allows former employees to join or start competitors but still provides a legal framework for the protection of proprietary secrets.

The value of a NCA in the context of a transaction is its ability to reduce the risk of business acquisitions by minimizing loss of employees, customers, and suppliers. For employers, NCAs can protect against employee and client poaching

Figure 23.1

Arguments In Favor of Non-Competes	Arguments Against Non-Competes
Non-competes prevent former employees from spreading business secrets	Non-competes stifle innovation by limiting competition
Non-competes prevent loss of key employees, customers, and suppliers	The first mover advantage should allow for enough profit
The new legislation would undermine the state's reputation, as it reneges on contracts by overturning case law supporting non-competes	Employees are often not made aware of non-compete agreements until after they have accepted the job

when employees leave for a competitor. When valuing a NCA, an analyst would consider the impact of competition (amount and duration) projected into the future, multiplied by the likelihood of competition (ability and willingness), discounted back to the present at an appropriate discount rate. Enforceability has always been an issue with NCAs, but threat of action is often enough to prevent a seller or former employee from reentering the market. This new legislation would highly limit the enforceability of employee NCA's and could bring NCA's in buy-sell agreements into question, removing any value of the former and potentially reducing the value of the latter.

While opinions are split, the winds of change may be blowing against covenants not to compete: California and North Dakota have already adopted similar policies and some data suggests that Massachusetts's inability to compete with its tech-rival California is because of its rival's freer labor market.[2]

End Notes

[1]   "Massachusetts Governor Proposed Sweeping Ledislation Banning Non-Compete Agreements,"https://www.lexology.com/library/detail.aspx?g=0cbd5604-5818-4a54-94ff-4859209f5185

[2]   "Patrick Looks to Eliminate Tech Non-Compete Agreements," http://www.betaboston.com/news/2014/04/10/patrick-looks-to-eliminate-tech-noncompete-agreements/

24

A Buyer's Market: Accounting for Bargain Purchases

Originally Published on December 20, 2013

A bargain purchase results when the fair value of the assets acquired exceeds the purchase price. If a transaction is determined to be bargain purchase, the acquirer must recognize a gain on its income statement.

The volatility of the commercial banking industry during the financial crisis resulted in a number of banks recognizing bargain purchase gains as they acquired distressed banks. Indeed, as industries undergo cyclical changes and consolidation trends, the likelihood of strategic buyers recognizing a bargain purchase gain increases.

Bargain purchases can be the result of a distressed seller or the lack of recognition of a contingent liability. Bargain purchases can also result when an earnout was part of the purchase consideration, but sufficient information is not available in order to recognize a contingent liability, thus leading to a disconnect between purchase accounting and the economic reality of a transaction.

In order to determine whether or not a transaction can be categorized as a bargain purchase, the original valuation and identification of identifiable assets and liabilities (including intangibles) must be reassessed.

ASC 805-30-30-5 states that the required reassessment should include a review of all of the following:

- The identifiable assets acquired and liabilities assumed

- The noncontrolling interest in the acquiree, if any

- For a business combination achieved in stages, the acquirer's previously held interest in the acquiree

- The consideration transferred

Reviewing the methodologies and assumptions used in the initial purchase price allocation to value intangible assets and contingent liabilities is a crucial step in determining whether or not a transaction meets the criteria to be categorized as a bargain purchase. The valuation of such assets and liabilities must reflect all available information at the acquisition date.

Portfolio Valuation

25

Marking Illiquid Investments in Liquid Funds

Travis W. Harms, CFA, CPA/ABV
Originally Published on March 14, 2016

As mutual fund flows continue to favor passive strategies, some active fund managers are beginning to look to alternative asset classes to augment returns and generate sustainable alpha. Since open-end funds need to calculate NAV on a daily basis, the inclusion of illiquid venture capital investments in liquid funds shines a brighter spotlight on fair value measurement.

Fund giant Fidelity has garnered the most attention for their venture capital fair value marks.[1,2] Figure 25.1 summarizes relevant data for a sample of investment holdings in 27 venture companies held by the Fidelity Growth Company Fund (FDGRX).[3]

At the end of January 2016, the reported fair value of the Level 3 venture investments on Figure 25.1 totaled $730.7 million, or 2.0% of total fund assets at that date.[4] We offer the following observations:

- It is clear that a fair value process is being followed. While the range of reasonableness for these investments can be wider than what is typical for more liquid investments, Fidelity does not appear to be allowing fair values to become stale. Of the 34 individual positions in the sample, 23 reported changes in fair value during the two months between November 30, 2015 and January 29, 2016.

Figure 25.1: Fidelity Growth Company Fund Level 3 Fair Value Marks (in $millions)

		Shares Owned	Purchase Date	Purchase Cost	FV Marks 5/31/15	FV Marks 11/30/15	FV Marks 1/29/16
Appirio, Inc.	Common	389,363	Feb-15	$2.78	$2.78	$1.75	$1.65
Appirio, Inc.	E	2,725,544	Feb-15	19.46	19.46	12.27	11.56
AppNexus, Inc.	E	923,523	Aug-14	18.50	23.71	18.54	14.79
Apptio, Inc.	E	881,266	May-13	20.00	18.25	17.22	14.68
Azul-Linhas	B	1,017,079	Dec-13	43.14	38.30	31.55	38.14
Azul-Linhas	Warrants	1,017,079	Dec-13	0.00	0.00	0.00	0.00
BeiGene	A2	8,617,681	Apr-15	10.08	10.08	10.08	11.03
Blue Apron	D	750,363	May-15	10.00	10.00	10.00	9.47
C. Wonder	A-1	619,048	Dec-12	19.50	0.00	0.00	0.00
Cloudera	F	529,285	Feb-14	7.71	11.28	17.38	17.38
CloudFlare	D	1,429,726	Nov-14	8.76	8.91	10.07	6.99
Dataminr	D	1,773,901	Feb-15	22.62	22.62	15.33	14.08
Domo	D	2,990,903	Jan-14	12.36	25.22	24.74	21.24
Dropbox	Common	1,105,082	May-12	10.00	18.12	14.92	13.31
Intarcia	CC	1,051,411	Nov-12	14.33	32.72	32.72	32.72
Intarcia	DD	1,543,687	Mar-14	50.00	48.04	48.04	48.04
Kolltan Pharma	D	7,940,644	Mar-14	7.94	7.94	7.94	7.94
Moderna	D	468,823	Nov-13	10.00	28.91	28.91	21.69
Moderna	E	565,117	Dec-14	34.85	34.85	34.85	26.14
MongoDB	F	1,913,404	Oct-13	32.00	16.74	14.89	13.36
Nutanix	E	1,151,309	Aug-14	15.42	18.05	18.17	14.28
Roku	F	17,901,305	May-13	16.21	21.48	27.37	27.37
Roku	G	2,750,007	Oct-14	3.57	3.30	4.20	4.20
RPI International		84,791	May-15	10.00	10.00	11.69	11.89
Snapchat	F	452,473	Mar-15	13.90	13.90	11.88	11.65
SpaceX	G	216,276	Jan-15	16.75	16.75	19.25	19.25
Syros Pharma	B	3,779,290	Oct-14	11.89	11.89	11.89	14.34
Taboola	E	1,337,420	Dec-14	13.94	13.94	9.51	10.86
The Honest Co	Common	39,835	Aug-14	1.08	1.17	1.82	1.82
The Honest Co	C	92,950	Aug-14	2.52	2.73	4.25	4.25
Turn Inc	E	984,774	Dec-13	8.21	6.10	3.64	3.40
Uber	D	4,770,180	Jun-14	74.40	158.93	189.09	232.65
Uber	E	209,216	Dec-14	6.97	6.97	8.29	10.20
YourPeople (Zenefits)	C	5,833,137	May-15	86.92	86.92	48.82	40.31
Sample Total				$635.8	$750.1	$721.1	$730.7

Source: Fidelity Growth Company Fund Annual Report (11/30/15), Semi-Annual Report (5/31/15) and Portfolio Holdings Listing (1/29/16)

Portfolio Valuation

Figure 25.1: Fidelity Growth Company Fund Level 3 Fair Value Marks (in $millions) (continued)

	FV Marks / Cost			Change in FV Marks			1/29/16 Holding Period	Annualized Return
	5/31/15	11/30/15	1/29/16	11/30/15	1/29/16	Cumulative		
Appirio, Inc.	1.00x	0.63x	0.59x	-37.0%	-5.8%	-40.6%	0.96	-41.8%
Appirio, Inc.	1.00x	0.63x	0.59x	-37.0%	-5.8%	-40.6%	0.96	-41.8%
AppNexus, Inc.	1.28x	1.00x	0.80x	-21.8%	-20.2%	-37.6%	1.50	-13.9%
Apptio, Inc.	0.91x	0.86x	0.73x	-5.6%	-14.7%	-19.6%	2.74	-10.7%
Azul-Linhas	0.89x	0.73x	0.88x	-17.6%	20.9%	-0.4%	2.10	-5.7%
Azul-Linhas	1.00x	1.00x	1.00x	0.0%	0.0%	0.0%	2.10	0.0%
BeiGene	1.00x	1.00x	1.09x	0.0%	9.4%	9.4%	0.78	12.3%
Blue Apron	1.00x	1.00x	0.95x	0.0%	-5.3%	-5.3%	0.70	-7.5%
C. Wonder	0.00x	0.00x	0.00x	0.0%	0.0%	0.0%	3.09	-99.2%
Cloudera	1.46x	2.25x	2.25x	54.0%	0.0%	54.0%	1.98	50.7%
CloudFlare	1.02x	1.15x	0.80x	13.1%	-30.6%	-21.5%	1.23	-16.7%
Dataminr	1.00x	0.68x	0.62x	-32.2%	-8.1%	-37.7%	0.95	-39.4%
Domo	2.04x	2.00x	1.72x	-1.9%	-14.1%	-15.8%	2.01	30.8%
Dropbox	1.81x	1.49x	1.33x	-17.7%	-10.8%	-26.6%	3.75	7.9%
Intarcia	2.28x	2.28x	2.28x	0.0%	0.0%	0.0%	3.21	29.3%
Intarcia	0.96x	0.96x	0.96x	0.0%	0.0%	0.0%	1.87	-2.1%
Kolltan Pharma	1.00x	1.00x	1.00x	0.0%	0.0%	0.0%	1.88	0.0%
Moderna	2.89x	2.89x	2.17x	0.0%	-25.0%	-25.0%	2.23	41.5%
Moderna	1.00x	1.00x	0.75x	0.0%	-25.0%	-25.0%	1.12	-22.7%
MongoDB	0.52x	0.47x	0.42x	-11.1%	-10.3%	-20.2%	2.33	-31.3%
Nutanix	1.17x	1.18x	0.93x	0.6%	-21.4%	-20.9%	1.43	-5.3%
Roku	1.33x	1.69x	1.69x	27.4%	0.0%	27.4%	2.73	21.1%
Roku	0.92x	1.18x	1.18x	27.4%	0.0%	27.4%	1.33	13.1%
RPI International	1.00x	1.17x	1.19x	16.9%	1.7%	18.9%	0.69	28.4%
Snapchat	1.00x	0.85x	0.84x	-14.5%	-1.9%	-16.2%	0.85	-18.8%
SpaceX	1.00x	1.15x	1.15x	14.9%	0.0%	14.9%	1.02	14.5%
Syros Pharma	1.00x	1.00x	1.21x	0.0%	20.6%	20.6%	1.31	15.4%
Taboola	1.00x	0.68x	0.78x	-31.8%	14.2%	-22.1%	1.10	-20.2%
The Honest Co	1.09x	1.69x	1.69x	55.5%	0.0%	55.5%	1.44	44.0%
The Honest Co	1.09x	1.69x	1.69x	55.8%	0.0%	55.8%	1.44	44.0%
Turn Inc	0.74x	0.44x	0.41x	-40.3%	-6.8%	-44.3%	2.08	-34.5%
Uber	2.14x	2.54x	3.13x	19.0%	23.0%	46.4%	1.65	99.6%
Uber	1.00x	1.19x	1.46x	19.0%	23.0%	46.4%	1.15	39.3%
YourPeople (Zenefits)	1.00x	0.56x	0.46x	-43.8%	-17.4%	-53.6%	0.75	-64.2%
Sample Total	1.18x	1.13x	1.15x	-14.0%	13.2%	-2.6%	1.58	9.2%

- Fidelity disregards a prominent tenet of the reigning fair value ortho-doxy, which is that the fair value of shares within a complex capital structure must take into account the unique economic rights and attri-butes of the individual classes. In the sample of investments presented in Figure 25.1, the fund owns multiples securities in seven enterprises (the shaded rows). With the single exception of a warrant in Azul-Linhas, the fair value marks are identical, on a per share basis, for the different classes. This outcome is consistent with determining the fair value of the enterprise and dividing by the fully-diluted share count.

  In our experience, this approach reflects the thinking of actual venture investors (who, presumably, count as market participants). Auditors, on the other hand, tend in our experience to require using a probability-weighted expected return method or option pricing method to allocate enterprise value to the various classes. While this technique is theoretically superior, it is in conflict with market par-ticipant perspectives on value. Since fair value is explicitly a market participant concept, this raises an interesting philosophical issue: how should fair value incorporate market participant perspectives with regard to valuation techniques? The fund's financial statements are audited by a Big 4 firm. Clear, uniform guidance around this issue would be most helpful to both reporting entities and fair value mea-surement specialists.

- Non-systematic factors are a significant component of fair value mea-surement. While the sample is admittedly small, the observed changes in fair value bear no discernible relationship to changes in the Nasdaq composite.

  For venture companies, operational and developmental milestones drive value much more than overall market performance and near-term economic data.

- The venture investments were accretive to net asset value per share during the period. Compared to the cumulative loss of 2.3% on the ven-ture investments, the aggregate NAV per share for the fund declined 13.9% over the same period.

Figure 25.2: Appirio, Inc. Fair Value Marks

$ millions, at January 29, 2016

	Fair Value	Shares	FV per Share
Common Shares	$1.7	389,363	$4.24
Series E Preferred Share	$11.6	2,725,544	$4.24

Chart 25.1: Performance Relative to Nasdaq

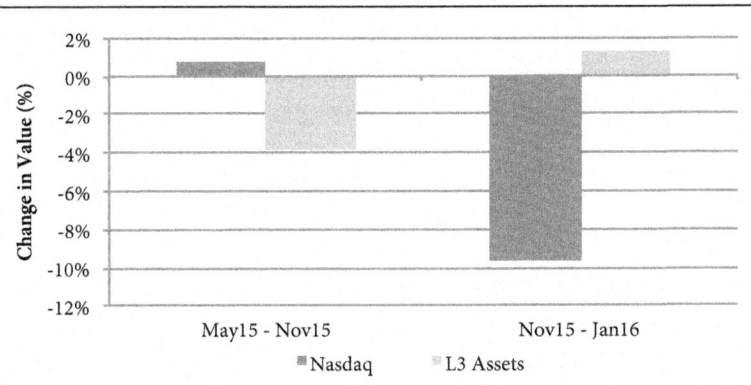

Chart 25.2: Dispersion of Returns

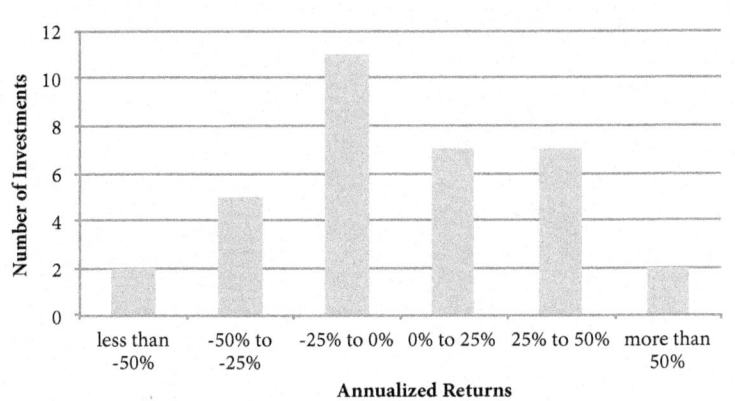

• Calculated from the respective investment dates, the venture investments have posted an aggregate annualized return of 9.2%. The dispersion of results for individual investments has been quite wide, however.

Of the 35 individual positions in the portfolio, sixteen have generated annualized returns (positive and negative) in excess of 25%. Venture investing is not
for the faint of heart. The fund's investment in Uber has performed quite well
(99.6% annualized return for Series D and 39.3% for Series E). Without Uber,
the overall return on the venture portfolio decreases from 9.2% to negative 7.8%.

Whether venture investing on the part of mutual fund managers is ultimately
a good idea is a topic for another day. However, the fair value disclosures surrounding such investments are a treasure trove of information for curious
observers. The disclosures bring a measure of transparency to the fair value
results for a respected market participant within an asset class for which fair
value inputs are difficult to support with precision.

End Notes

[1] Available online: http://fortune.com/2015/11/12/fidelity-marks-down-tech-unicorns/

[2] Available online: http://www.bloomberg.com/news/articles/2016-03-01/fidelity-writes-down-value-of-corporate-software-startups

[3] Available online: https://fundresearch.fidelity.com/mutual-funds/summary/316200104

[4] We excluded investments made subsequent to May 31, 2015 from the table to enhance comparability over time. Including such investments, Level 3 assets at November 30, 2015 totaled $1.2 billion, or 2.4% of total assets at that date. The Portfolio Holdings Listing at January 29, 2016 does not segregate Level 3 assets.

26

Are You GIPS-Compliant?

Mary Grace McQuiston
Originally Published on January 4, 2016

The Global Investment Performance Standards (GIPS®) were adopted by the CFA Institute in 1999 and are widely accepted among the international investment management industry.[1] GIPS are a set of ethical principles based on a standardized, industry-wide approach that apply to investment management firms and are intended to serve prospective and existing clients of investment firms. While compliance by investment firms is voluntary, many investors consider GIPS compliance to be a requirement for doing business with an investment manager. Alternative managers have lagged behind the industry in claiming compliance with GIPS, but changes in the industry suggest GIPS compliance is becomingly increasingly important.

On the CFA Institute *Market Integrity Insights* blog, Beth Kaiser identifies two reasons GIPS compliance is becoming increasingly important, specifically for alternative investment managers. One driver is that alternative strategies are becoming increasingly mainstream and investors and consultants are engaging in more comprehensive due diligence. Compliance with GIPS can help managers to stand out amongst their peers. Furthermore, the issuance of the GIPS Guidance Statement on Alternative Investment Strategies in 2012 makes it easier for alternative investment managers to comply.

The GIPS Guidance Statement on Alternative Strategies and Structures specifically addresses compliance for hedge funds and other alternative investment strategies.[2] GIPS standards state that portfolios must be valued in accordance with the definition of fair value and that all investments, regardless of liquidity, must have valuations that adhere to the definition of fair value. In addition, firms are to disclose if pricing has been performed internally and not by an external third party.

At the 2015 GIPS Annual Conference, it was revealed that the California Public Employees' Retirement System (CalPERS) inquires of all investment managers, including alternative investment managers, seeking to do business with them whether they are GIPS-compliant.[3] The position of CalPERS in the industry suggests that managers will take the steps necessary to win its business and that GIPS-compliance is quickly becoming the norm for investment managers.

End Notes

[1] Available online: https://www.cfainstitute.org/learning/products/publications/ccb/Pages/ccb.v2012.n4.full.aspx

[2] Available online: https://www.gipsstandards.org/standards/Documents/Guidance/gs_alternative_investment_strategies_and_structures.pdf

[3] Available online: https://blogs.cfainstitute.org/marketintegrity/2015/11/10/gips-and-alternatives-calpers-takes-notice-others-likely-to-follow/

27

A Few Thoughts on Valuing Investments in Startups: An Interview with Travis Harms

Sujan Rajbhandary, CFA
Originally Published on November 6, 2015

Recently, we interviewed Travis Harms, who leads the financial reporting valuation practice at Mercer Capital. Travis commented on a few issues around valuations of startups from a financial reporting perspective. The following is a lightly edited transcript.

Please tell us a little bit about yourself and your practice at Mercer Capital.

I joined Mercer Capital in 1999. For the past ten years, I've had the privilege of leading our financial statement reporting team. Our group helps clients tackle some of the thornier fair value-related questions that arise in the context of financial reporting. For public companies and larger privates, goodwill impairment testing and measuring the value of identifiable assets for purchase price allocation are the most common assignments. For private equity funds and other financial sponsors, we provide equity compensation valuations for both GAAP reporting and tax, or 409a, compliance. Finally, we assist investment funds in developing reliable fair value marks for illiquid portfolio holdings.

With respect to portfolio valuation, who are your clients and what services do you provide?

In our portfolio valuation practice, clients cover the spectrum from debt-focused funds, to hedge funds, traditional private equity funds, venture funds, and sector-focused credit and equity funds. Despite the diversity of strategies, what they all have in common is the need to develop reliable, defensible fair value marks for hard-to-value assets in a real-time reporting cycle.

That reporting cycle varies by client – we mark some assets on a monthly basis, while we look at others annually. The frequency with which we mark assets is generally a function of the fund manager's ability to develop interim marks on their own – do they have the requisite expertise and staffing to develop and document reasonable interim marks?

Now, of course, the fund manager has the expertise to value assets. However, the fund manager's valuation objective is to determine "intrinsic" or "investment" value, which may well differ from the prevailing market consensus. That is not the objective of fair value reporting, though. Fair value is not the fund manager's price target based on his investment thesis. It is a particularly defined standard: fair value is the price that would be received to sell an asset in an orderly transaction between market participants at the measurement date. Developing and documenting the corresponding market participant inputs can be time-consuming and requires a different perspective than the fund manager is accustomed to using.

Sometimes we are developing our own independent estimates of fair value from scratch; other times we are examining the fund manager's own estimates for the purpose of providing positive assurance that the marks are reasonable. Regardless of the scope of our work, documenting, presenting, and defending our conclusions to auditors and, potentially, regulators is always part of our job.

Looking to the VC markets a bit, you have commented on the Unicorn phenomenon and suggested that from a valuation perspective, "What's obvious isn't real, what's real isn't obvious." What do you mean?

What we mean is that, while the headline valuation ascribed to a company following a fundraising round is obvious (price x fully-diluted shares outstanding), that is not the real value of the company. What is less obvious, but considerably more real, is that the price per share in the most recent round reflects all of the rights and economic attributes of that share class. Those rights and attributes are not the same for all of the other shares included in the fully diluted share count. It's like applying the per-pound price for filet mignon to the entire cow – you can't do that because the cow includes a lot of other stuff that is not filet. In the same way, the "obvious" pxq calculation overstates the value of an early-stage company. Now, no doubt the values of many "unicorns" are substantial, even when calculated correctly – but the real values are not nearly as obvious as the often breathless headlines would suggest.

Last week, a Wall Street Journal article elaborated on some of the difficulties that mutual funds face in valuing their investments in startups.[1] Based on your experience with providing periodic fair value marks for VC funds, what are some of the elements that go into valuing such investments? What are some of the pain points?

Valuing startup investments, including "unicorns" such as those mentioned in the Wall Street Journal article, requires developing a thorough understanding of the economics of the most recent funding round, which provides a market-based "anchor" for valuation at subsequent measurement dates. What we find most effective is to build our valuation model so that it corroborates the "anchor" value as of the date of the most recent external funding round. Once our model is appropriately calibrated, we can then develop appropriate market participant model inputs for the measurement date that take into account changes in markets, company performance, and prospects for future exit with regard to timing, amount, and form.

Valuing these investments is particularly challenging given the illiquidity of the securities. When observable transactions occur only sporadically or at long intervals, it can be difficult to assess how changes in the market and company prospects will influence value. The longer the holding period – in other words, as you move from days to months to years – the greater the uncertainty regarding reasonable inputs and the wider the range of potential outcomes. Things become even more difficult when you layer in the unique features of many of these securities, such as liquidation preference, conversion, participation, and other rights and features.

Finally, the WSJ article discusses the fact that there is variation, sometimes substantial, in the valuation marks provided by different investors in the same company. Is that troublesome?

Is it troubling that different reasonably informed investment professionals come to different good faith estimates of the fair value of the securities we've been discussing? No. As we mentioned previously, illiquidity necessarily increases uncertainty. This is a phenomenon that you can observe even in securities that trade in markets – the less liquid and shallower the market, the wider the bid-ask spread will be. Even if you follow a rigorous calibration process like we outlined earlier, there is uncertainty about inputs. For example, you may know – on the basis of an observed market transaction – that a company's value was $40 at a particular date, but what you still cannot directly observe is whether that was 8 times 5 or 10 times 4. Those unobservable inputs will necessarily breed good faith differences of opinion as the $40 value becomes stale with the passage of time. That is not to say that anything goes – there is a range of reasonable conclusions. But no, different estimates of fair value for these securities are not in themselves troubling.

Whether it is troubling – given this valuation uncertainty – that an open-end mutual fund owns such securities is for the regulators to decide. It may be that the fair value estimates are reasonable, and reasonably different, but those differences are simply not tolerable from a regulatory standpoint. That, however, is ultimately not a valuation question.

End Note

[1]   Available online: http://www.wsj.com/articles/mutual-funds-flail-at-valuing-hot-startups-like-uber-1446174018

28

Turning on the Fasten Seat Belt Sign: Fair Value Measurement in Turbulence

Travis W. Harms, CFA, CPA/ABV
Originally Published on October 9, 2015

We have previously noted that the degree of difficulty for fair value measurements has been low for some time. Switching metaphors, choppy equity markets and widening credit spreads during the third quarter of 2015 indicate that it may no longer be safe to move about the valuation cabin.

Chart 28.1: Fair Value of Benchmark Debt Instrument

Terms of Benchmark Loan	Valuation Assumption
Expected Term: 4 years	Market Participant Spread adjusts with BAML
Spread to LIBOR: 900 bps	High Yield B OAS
LIBOR Floor: 100 bps	
Call Price: 103	

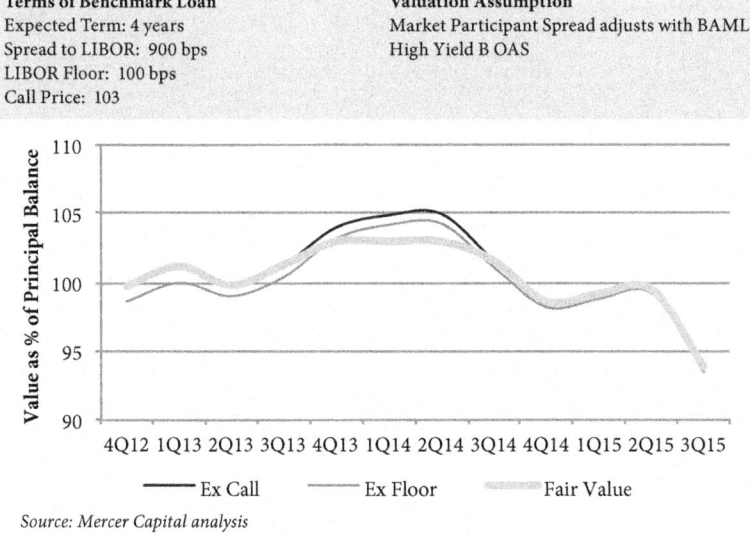

Source: Mercer Capital analysis

Figure 28.1

	Fourth Quarter 2014			Third Quarter 2015		
	Beginning	End	Widening	Beginning	End	Widening
BAML High Yield Master II OAS	440	504	64	500	662	162
BAML U.S. High Yield Energy OAS	453	756	303	712	1,098	386
Implied Ex-Energy	438	460	22	463	585	122

Chart 28.2

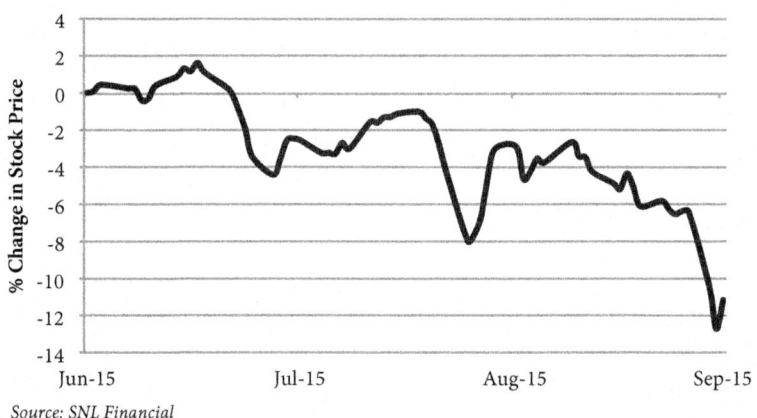

Source: SNL Financial

A nearly 200 basis point increase in the BofA Merrill Lynch US High Yield B Option-Adjusted Spread during the quarter pushed the fair value of our benchmark loan from 99.5 to 93.9, as shown in Chart 28.2.

As was the case in 4Q14, energy credits led the way down. However, unlike 4Q14, the spread widening was much broader. Assuming that energy credits account for approximately 15% of the high yield universe, non-energy spreads widened 122 basis points during the third quarter.

For business development companies and many other debt-focused funds, the use of financial leverage magnifies the pressure on net asset value from wider credit spreads. Using our benchmark loan as a proxy for the fair value of port-folio assets, the 5.6% decline in the value of portfolio assets translates into a 9.4% decrease in net assets for a fund with 40% leverage. As evident below, BDC investors seem to be taking a similar – perhaps even a bit dimmer – view of portfolio values, as stock prices fell about 11% during the quarter.

Widening credit spreads ultimately signal market concerns about credit quality. While reported credit statistics for BDCs and other non-traditional lenders have remained robust so far in this cycle, the market signals suggest that lenders are likely to begin disclosing less healthy portfolio credit metrics. Measuring the fair value of individual credits in such an environment becomes even more difficult as one must evaluate not only market-wide inputs, but also closely scrutinize the financial results and prospects of each borrower. Those assessments are difficult to make in real-time. For highly leveraged structured products like CLO equity, the sensitivity of a given fair value measurement to changes in inputs can be substantial.

The growing list of valuation-related litigation and enforcement actions is a tes-tament to the fact that fair value reporting matters. Valuation disputes are a portion – but by no means all – of the controversy surrounding the Zohar funds managed by Patriarch Partners LLC.[1]

Whether the third quarter represents merely a small patch of rough air or the beginning of a long, bumpy multi-quarter ride remains to be seen. In either event, it is a reminder that fair value measurement is not always so easy.

End Note

[1] Available online: http://www.wsj.com/articles/lynn-tilton-and-patriarch-partners-sued-over-investors-losses-1444084334

29

Unicorn Valuations:
What's Obvious Isn't Real, and
What's Real Isn't Obvious

Travis W. Harms, CFA, CPA/ABV
Originally Published on September 11, 2015

In the two short years since Aileen Lee introduced the term "unicorn " into the VC parlance, the number of such companies has steadily increased from the 39 identified by Lee's team at Cowboy Ventures to nearly 150 (and growing weekly) by most current estimates.[1] Pundits and analysts have offered a variety of explanations for the phenomenon, with some identifying unicorns as the sign that the tech bubble of the late 1990s has returned under a different guise, others attributing the existence of such companies to structural changes in how innovation is funded in the economy, and the most intrepid of the group suggesting that the previously undreamt valuations are fully supported by the underlying fundamentals given the maturity and ubiquity of the internet, smart phones, tablets, and related technologies.

We suspect there is merit to each of these perspectives. As valuation analysts, however, what sets our hearts atwitter is the very definition of "unicorn", which is predicated on valuation. Since companies are christened unicorns upon closing a financing round, one would assume valuation to be self-evident. Alas, that is generally far from the case. Because of the common features of VC investments, the "headline" valuation numbers are not reliable measures of the market value of the underlying enterprises. As a result, the frequent breathless comparisons of the value of startup X to publicly traded stalwart Y are often overblown and potentially misleading.

Figure 29.1

	Proceeds	Price	Shares	Issue Date
Series E	$175,000,000	$5.00	35,000,000	9/1/15
Series D	$60,000,000	$3.00	20,000,000	9/1/14
Series C	$25,000,000	$0.63	40,000,000	9/1/13
Series B	$7,500,000	$0.40	18,750,000	9/1/12
Series A	$5,250,000	$0.15	35,000,000	9/1/11
Total Preferred	$272,750,000		148,750,000	
Common Shares			51,250,000	9/1/10
Total Fully-Diluted Shares			**200,000,000**	

Consider the following example. The capitalization of a hypothetical freshly-minted unicorn, BlueCo, is summarized in Figure 29.1.

With 200 million fully-diluted shares post issuance, the $5.00 per share Series E offering results in a headline valuation of $1.0 billion (on a pre-money basis, BlueCo's headline valuation is $825 million). But is BlueCo really worth $1 billion? In other words, what does the Series E investment imply about the value of the stakes in BlueCo held by other investors?

The value of the whole is equal to the sum of the individual parts. So, for BlueCo to truly be worth $1 billion, all 200 million fully-diluted shares must be worth $5.00 each. But the various share classes are not created equal. At each subsequent funding stage, investors in startup companies negotiate terms to provide downside protection to their investment while preserving the upside potential if the subject company turns out to be a home run. Such provisions commonly include some or all of the following:

- Liquidation preferences that put the latest investors at the front of the line for exit proceeds. This is especially advantageous in the event the Company fails to meet expectations (basically LIFO treatment: the last one in is the first one out).

- Cumulative dividend rights that cause the liquidation preference to increase over time. When such rights are present, the preferred investors not only stand at the front of the line, but are entitled to a return on their investment if there are sufficient proceeds.

- Anti-dilution or ratchet provisions that allow preferred investors to hit the reset button on many of their economic rights in the event the company is forced to raise money in the future at a lower price.

- Participation rights that allow the preferred investors to simultaneously benefit from the payoff to common shares while also recovering their initial investment via liquidation preference.

A recent *New York Times* article highlighted additional, more exotic rights and privileges being attached to recent financings.[2]

For the sake of illustration, we will assume that the terms of BlueCo's Series E preferred shares are generally favorable to the other investors: pro rata liquidation preference to other preferred investors, non-cumulative dividends, and no participation rights. Despite these relatively benign terms, owning Class E shares is clearly preferable to owning more junior classes. Consider the waterfall of proceeds under various strategic sale exit scenarios:

Figure 29.2

	$400 million Exit		$800 million Exit		$1.2 billion Exit	
	Total Proceeds	Per Share	Total Proceeds	Per Share	Total Proceeds	Per Share
Series E	$175,000,000	$5.00	$175,000,000	$5.00	$210,000,000	$6.00
Series D	$60,000,000	$3.00	$75,757,576	$3.79	$120,000,000	$6.00
Series C	$45,517,241	$1.14	$151,515,152	$3.79	$240,000,000	$6.00
Series B	$21,336,207	$1.14	$71,022,727	$3.79	$112,500,000	$6.00
Series A	$39,827,586	$1.14	$132,575,758	$3.79	$210,000,000	$6.00
Total Preferred	$341,681,034		$605,871,212		$892,500,000	
Common Shares	$58,318,966	$1.14	$194,128,788	$3.79	$307,500,000	$6.00
Total	**$400,000,000**		**$800,000,000**		**$1,200,000,000**	

Even under the relatively disappointing $400 million exit scenario, the Scenario E shareholders are entitled to return of their investment, or $5.00 per share, while the proceeds to more subordinate classes range from $1.14 per share to $3.00 per share. Chart 29.1 depicts the superiority of the proceeds for Series E preferred shares to Series A shares over enterprise exit values less than $1.0 billion.

The area between the payoff lines for Class E and Class A preferred shares represents the incremental value available to the more senior Class E shares. Borrowing from the fair value measurement lexicon, if the recent Series E issuance price of $5.00 per share is consonant with market participant expectations, then that same group of market participants would rationally assign a lower value to the Class A shares. Valuation analysts use two primary techniques for estimating the magnitude of the difference in share value across the various classes. Examining the relative merits of the two techniques (the probability-weighted expected return method, or PWERM, and the option pricing method, or OPM) is beyond the scope of this blog post. Both models are reasonably intuitive but require numerous assumptions for which irrefutable support can prove elusive.

We use the OPM to illustrate the impact of the rights and preferences of the most senior preferred shareholders on the economic value of a nominal unicorn. The two most subjective assumptions in the OPM are the time remaining

Chart 29.1

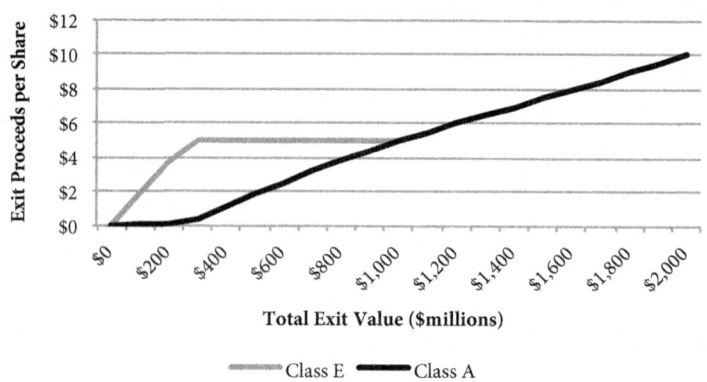

until exit and the return volatility of the underlying business. The sensitivity table below depicts the implied total enterprise value of BlueCo (that would reconcile to the $5.00 per Series E preferred share transaction price) using the OPM under a range of assumptions for exit timing, given assumed volatility of 100%:

Over the range of exit timing assumptions noted above, the implied total enterprise value ranges from less than $600 million to just over $800 million, mean-

Figure 29.3: OPM-Implied Enterprise Values at Series E Issuance ($millions)

Volatility	Estimated Time to Exit		
	0.5 Years	3 Years	5 Years
100%	$592	$748	$822

ingful discounts to the $1 billion headline number. The reliability of the OPM and the assumed inputs can be debated; however the point remains that, since the subordinate classes are necessarily worth less than Series E, the total enterprise value is less than $1 billion.

So what?

Is the preceding analysis just so much valuation pedantry? Perhaps, but we suggest that these observations reflect one practical peril of high valuations for late stage investors and management teams. The implied enterprise value based on rights and preferences of senior investors is relevant precisely because buyers in the exit markets for start-up companies – strategic sales and IPOs – assess the value of the entire enterprise, not individual interests. The exit markets assign a value for the entire company, exhibiting a serene indifference to how that value is allocated to various investors. This can result in unflattering headlines and unpleasant outcomes for late stage investors.

Let's return to the BlueCo example to illustrate. Assume that the appropriate assumptions for BlueCo from the sensitivity table above are three years to exit,

Figure 29.4

	Implied Enterprise Value		$975 million Strategic Sale		Realized Return
	Total Value	Per Share	Total Proceeds	Per Share	
Series E	$175,000,000	$5.00	$175,000,000	$5.00	0.0%
Series D	$83,916,440	$4.19	$96,969,697	$4.85	15.7%
Series C	$138,185,693	$3.45	$193,939,394	$4.85	40.5%
Series B	$63,823,193	$3.40	$90,909,091	$4.85	42.6%
Series A	$117,302,036	$3.35	$169,696,970	$4.85	44.7%
Total Preferred	$578,227,362		$726,515,152		
Common Shares	$170,236,414	$3.32	$248,484,848	$4.85	46.0%
Total	$748,463,776	30% increase in EV ➤	$975,000,000		

Figure 29.5

	Implied Enterprise Value		$975 million IPO		Realized Return
	Total Value	Per Share	Total Proceeds	Per Share	
Series E	$175,000,000	$5.00	$170,625,000	$4.88	-2.5%
Series D	$83,916,440	$4.19	$97,500,000	$4.88	16.3%
Series C	$138,185,693	$3.45	$195,000,000	$4.88	41.3%
Series B	$63,823,193	$3.40	$91,406,250	$4.88	43.4%
Series A	$117,302,036	$3.35	$170,625,000	$4.88	45.5%
Total Preferred	$578,227,362		$726,515,152		
Common Shares	$170,236,414	$3.32	$249,843,750	$4.88	46.8%
Total	$748,463,776	30% increase in EV ➤	$975,000,000		

implying an enterprise value of $748 million. In the year following the Series E investment, BlueCo management executes its strategy successfully, causing the enterprise value to increase 30% to $975 million. If BlueCo exits via a strategic sale at that point, none of the incremental enterprise value will accrue to the Series E investors; despite identifying an attractive company, and the strong execution of management, the Series E investors will receive their capital back with no return.

If the exit occurs instead by IPO, things get even more awkward. In contrast to a strategic sale, an IPO is a pro rata exit, meaning that the realized return for the Series E preferred investors will actually be negative, despite the 30% increase in enterprise value. Further, the Company and its management team will likely be subject to some unfavorable press for executing a "downround" IPO, although in reality, it generated a handsome return for the investor group as a whole.

So when is a unicorn really a unicorn? We hesitate to draw a bright line; circumstances and assumptions vary. Regardless of size, the lesson for investors and management teams at early-stage companies is to beware the headline valuation number. Appearances can be deceiving.

End Notes

[1]   Available online: https://techcrunch.com/2013/11/02/welcome-to-the-unicorn-club/

[2]   Available online: http://www.nytimes.com/2015/06/08/business/dealbook/protections-for-late-investors-can-inflate-start-up-valuations.html?_r=0

30

How to Value Venture Capital Portfolio Investments

Sujan Rajbhandary, CFA
Originally Published on May 8, 2015

The blog post outlines our process when providing periodic fair value marks for venture capital fund investments in pre-public companies (see Figure 30.1 on the next page).

Examine the Most Recent Financing Round Economics

The transaction underlying the initiation of an investment position can provide three critical pieces of information from a valuation perspective:

- Size of the aggregate investment and per share price.

- Rights and protections accorded to the newest round of securities.

- Usually, but not always, an indication of the underlying enterprise value from the investor's perspective.

Deal terms commonly reported in the press focus on the size of the aggregate investment and per share price.[1] The term "valuation" is usually a headline-shorthand for implied post-money value that assumes all equity securities in the company's capital structure have identical rights and protections. While elegant, this approach glosses over the fact that for pre-public companies, securities with differing rights and protections should and do command different prices.

Figure 30.1

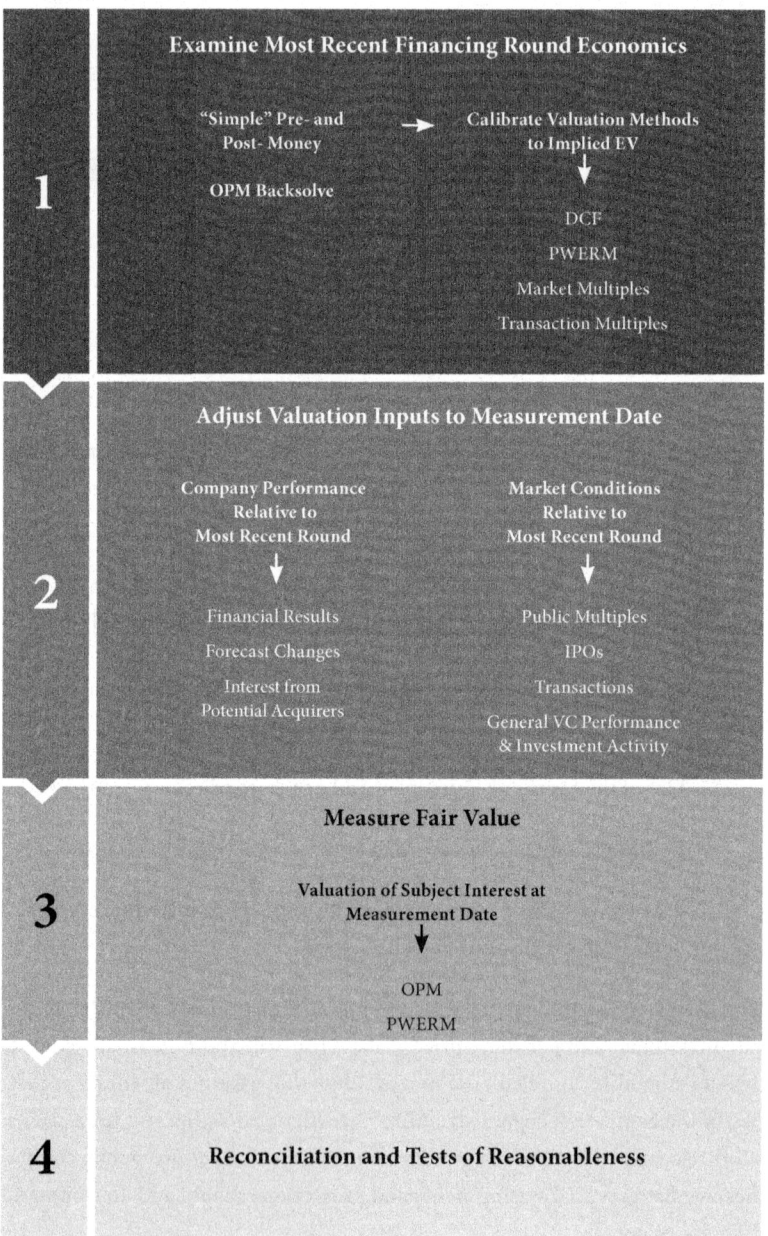

The option pricing method (OPM) is an alternative that explicitly models the rights of each equity class and makes generalized assumptions about the future trajectory of the company to deduce values for the various securities. Valuation specialists can also use the probability-weighted expected return method (PWERM) to evaluate potential proceeds from, and the likelihood of, several exit scenarios for a company. Total proceeds from each scenario would then be allocated to the various classes of equity based on their relative rights. The use of PWERM is particularly viable if there is sufficient visibility into the future exit prospects for the company.

The economics of the most recent financing round helps calibrate inputs used in both the OPM and PWERM.

- Under the OPM, a backsolve procedure provides indications of total equity and enterprise value based on the pricing and terms the most recent financing round. The indicated enterprise value and a set of future cash flow projections, taken together, imply a rate of return (discount rate) that may be reasonable for the company. Multiples implied by the indicated enterprise value, juxtaposed with information from publicly traded companies or related transactions, can yield valuation-useful inferences.

- Under the PWERM, in addition to informing discount rates and providing comparisons with market multiples, the most recent financing round can inform the relative likelihood of the various exit scenarios.

When available, indications of enterprise value from the investor's perspectives can further inform the inputs used in the various valuation methods.

In addition to the quantitative inputs enumerated above, discussions and documentation around the recent financing round can provide critical qualitative information, as well.

Adjust Valuation Inputs to Measurement Date

Between a funding round and subsequent measurement dates, the performance of the company and changes in market conditions can provide context for any adjustments that may be warranted for the valuation inputs. Deterioration in actual financial projections may warrant revisiting the set of projected cash flows, while improvements in market multiples for similar companies may suggest better pricing may be available for the company at exit. Interest from potential acquirers (or withdrawal of prior interest) and general IPO trends can inform inputs related to the relative likelihood of the various exit scenarios.

Measure Fair Value

Measuring fair value of the subject security entails using the OPM and PWERM, as appropriate and viable, in conjunction with valuation inputs that are relevant at the measurement date. ASC 820 defines fair value as, "The price that would be received to sell an asset or paid to transfer a liability in an orderly transaction between market participants at the measurement date."

Reconciliation and Tests of Reasonableness

A sanity check to scrutinize fair value outputs is an important element of the measurement process. Specifically as it relates to venture capital investments in pre-public companies, such a check would reconcile a fair value indication at the current measurement date with a mark from the prior period in light of both changes in the subject company, and changes in market conditions.

Mercer Capital assists a range of alternative investment funds, including venture capital firms, in periodically measuring the fair value of portfolio assets for financial reporting purposes to the satisfaction of the general partners and fund auditors. Call us – we would like to work with you to define appropriate fund valuation policies and procedures, and provide independent opinions of value.

End Note

[1]   Zenefits for example: http://blogs.wsj.com/digits/2015/05/06/zenefits-tagged-with-4-5-billion-valuation-after-just-two-years/

31

Spotting Young Talent: Belgian Football and VC Investments

Sujan Rajbhandary, CFA
Originally Published on April 11, 2014

Towards the end of 2013, the Belgian football club FC Racing Boxburg awarded 20-month old Bryce Brites a contract. Disbelieving commentary around the signing coalesced around the notion that the evaluation of tender sports talent is completely subjective.[1]

Similar incredulity appears to have greeted the valuations implied by transactions involving a couple of (virtually) pre-revenue start-up companies.

- Quora raises $80 million at near-unicorn valuation.

- Facebook buying WhatsApp is a desperate move.

Unlike sports scouting, assessments of start-ups can (should?) include both qualitative and quantitative elements. While the list is far from comprehensive or universally applicable, start up founders and investors may assess the following factors in pondering the value of an opportunity.

- **Likelihood of technical viability.** Many, if not all, new ventures begin in the hopes of either tackling an unsolved problem or finding a better way to address current practices. Before a product or service can launch into the wider market, however, a new technology has to be viable. A social media company needs to be able to attract users and keep them engaged, and a medical technology start-up has to pass regulatory hurdles to develop an approved product. While feasibility may be mostly indeterminate for seed-stage ventures, the likelihood of technical viability usually becomes clearer as a start-up makes progress in achieving its milestones.

- **Total addressable market** reflects the scope of the unsolved problem or current practices that can be disrupted. Again, for many start-ups the size of the addressable market becomes clearer as they progress from early-stage to later stages. Even after product launch, strong platforms may be able to annex related market segments to expand the size of the addressable market. An online bookseller can morph over time to become a dominant retailer that also provides enterprise technology infrastructure.

- **Market share.** In a competitive economy, even the most convincing product or service may (should?) be able to garner only a fraction of the total addressable market. Market share will depend on the strength of the offered feature-set, as well as the ability to communicate the appeal of the products and services to potential customers.

- **Profitability**, or the efficiency with which a given dollar of revenue translates into profits, determines the cash flow potential of a business. The value of an enterprise, at least over the long run, is rooted in the amount of cash that can flow from the company to its shareholders.

- **Investments** necessary to achieve technical viability and execute market launch to sell products or services profitably at some future date.

- **Barriers to entry.** A useful technology may confer economic value to a particular owner or developer only to the extent it is not easily replicable. Intellectual property protection in the form of patents and trade names can deter competitors and preserve market share, as can regulatory approval requirements that can only be met via investments of time and money, and a bit of good luck.

- **Management quality.** Talent, hard work, ingenuity, grit – take your pick.

Inevitably, time will be the ultimate arbiter of whether each of the deals being struck at present will ever make sense. Investors with a portfolio of VC investments, however, may view an early funding round as a purchase of an option with a potential huge upside and limited downside.[2] In that sense, not all start-up companies need necessarily grow into their implied valuations for the portfolio of VC investments to be valuable.

Indeed, Belgian football also appears to have taken the portfolio approach to heart by setting up a number of youth academies around the country. For now, we will just have to wait 15 to 20 years to see if young Master Brites will someday light up the football pitch like his more illustrious compatriots, or turn out to be a proverbial flash in the pan.

End Notes

[1] Available online: http://bleacherreport.com/articles/1981917-birth-of-the-baby-footballer-at-what-age-can-you-spot-true-sporting-talent

[2] Available online: https://25iq.com/2014/03/29/the-fundamental-difference-between-venture-capital-and-value-investing/

32

Portfolio Valuation and Regulatory Scrutiny

Travis W. Harms, CFA, CPA/ABV
Originally Published on March 28, 2014

Over the past decade, we have been retained by several investment funds to assist them in responding to formal and informal SEC investigations regarding fair value measurement of portfolio investments. Reflecting back on those engagements yields a couple of observations and reminders for funds and fund managers as they go through the quarterly valuation process.

First, fund managers should recognize that valuation matters, and it will really matter when something has gone awry. To that end, we recommend that funds:

- **Document valuation procedures to follow (and follow them).** Since valuation requires judgment, disagreements are inevitable. However, are you following the established valuation process? In hindsight, judgments are especially susceptible to second-guessing if established policies and procedures are not followed.

- **Designate a member of senior management to be responsible for oversight of the valuation process.** Placing valuation under the purview of a senior member of management demonstrates that valuation is an important function, not a compliance afterthought.

- **Create contemporaneous and consistent documentation of valuation conclusions and rationale.** No valuation judgment is "too obvious" to merit being documented. On the other side of the next crisis, what seems reasonable today may appear anything but. The middle of an investigation is not the best time to re-construct rationales for prior valuation judgments.

Second, it is important for fund managers to stay abreast of evolving best practices (or know people who do). Fair value measurement for illiquid portfolio investments is an evolving discipline. We recommend that funds:

- **Solicit relevant input from the professionals responsible for the investment, auditors, and third-party valuation experts**. Relying on appropriate professionals demonstrates that the fund managers take compliance seriously and are committed to preparing reliable fair value measurements.

- **Check your math**. In the glare of the regulatory spotlight, few things will prove more embarrassing than elementary computational errors. The proverbial ounce of prevention is certainly worth the pound of cure.

- **Disclose the valuation process and conclusions**. Just like potential investors do, regulators take comfort in transparency.

The best time to prepare for a regulatory investigation is before it starts.

Equity Compensation

33

Why Quality Matters in Valuation for Equity Compensation Grants

Sujan Rajbhandary, CFA
Originally Published on April 3, 2015

For privately held companies (particularly those sponsored by private equity and venture capital funds), getting the valuation process right the first time for equity compensation grant compliance is always the least expensive route in terms of both direct and indirect cost.

- **Auditor Review.** The potential for surprises in the audit review process related to equity compensation is most significant with new auditors and for new equity compensation plans. It is not necessarily safe to assume that valuation procedures used in the past will be sufficient to pass the audit review process. Communication with auditors on the front end in this situation is paramount to make sure that valuation procedures (or the independent valuation provider) will be satisfactory. Valuation analysis is always more expensive when it has to be done twice.

- **SEC Scrutiny.** Preparing for an IPO is probably the worst time for a company to deal with fallout related to insufficient valuation procedures related to equity compensation. This situation quickly becomes very expensive. And the direct financial cost of compliance in this situation is often less burdensome than the distraction created at a time so close to the finish line when management most needs to be focused on execution of strategic objectives. For companies with even a distant prospect of IPO, robust valuation procedures for equity compensation compliance are necessary on the front-end.

- **IRS Review**. Even for companies not contemplating a potential IPO, the possible tax penalties from IRC 409A make defensible valuation analysis a priority. Further, there is limited case history to develop clear expectations of IRS scrutiny related to 409A compliance. We do know that IRS audits related to 409A have begun picking up, and it's likely that valuation reviews will follow suit. Drawing on our experience in other tax-related valuation matters, we know that thorough documentation and sound economic reasoning ultimately win the day. Given this uncertainty and magnitude of the consequences of 409A, it's best to play it safe.

In general, it is safe to expect the level of scrutiny over equity compensation-related valuation to increase with the size of the equity compensation grant – both the absolute magnitude (in terms of dollars) and relative magnitude (as a percentage of total revenue or enterprise value). While complexity of the equity compensation grant or capital structure does not inherently increase scrutiny, it does make it more challenging to demonstrate clear compliance with tax and financial reporting regulations. With appropriate awareness, management can minimize total compliance cost by selecting valuation procedures appropriate to the situation and getting it right the first time.

34

The IRS Equity Compensation Audit Guide

Samantha L. Albert
Originally Published on November 16, 2015

What do IRS examiners look for when auditing filings with equity-based compensation plans? The IRS recently released its *Equity (Stock)-Based Compensation Audit Techniques Guide*, which offers an opportunity to see how the IRS views equity-based compensation arrangements. The guide is intended to assist IRS examiners as well as to provide insight to corporate and individual taxpayers.

Scrutiny of 409A-related valuations has been increasing. Although case history remains limited, the new IRS guide helps to solidify expectations and highlights potential areas that the IRS might review. The guide is organized around the following areas:

- Summary of the various types of equity-based compensation

- Suggestions for examiners on where to find information on equity-based compensation plans, including SEC filings (annual filings, proxy statements, registration statements) and internal documents (employment contracts, meeting minutes, shareholder communications)

- Discussion of specific characteristics of stock transfers and the potential tax consequences associated with each type

- Potential issues involving statutory and non-statutory stock options

- Potential issues involving other types of equity-based compensation, including phantom stock plans, stock appreciation rights, restricted stock units, and stock warrants

Types of Equity-Based Compensation

The IRS guide discusses several types of equity-based compensation and comments on potential tax issues associated with each.

- **Statutory and Non-Statutory Options**. Statutory stock options, which include Incentive Stock Options ("ISOs") and options granted under an Employee Stock Purchase Plan, generally have stricter requirements than their non-statutory kin. For statutory options, exercise does not result in income or income tax obligations for the employee and the employer cannot take a corresponding deduction. Subject to certain conditions, when the stock is sold, the employee recognizes capital gains/losses on the stock equal to the lesser of (a) the excess of the fair market value ("FMV") of the stock on the date of disposition over the amount paid for the share and, (b) the excess of the share value on the option grant date over the exercise price. Non-statutory options result in ordinary income on the date of exercise. Non-statutory options with an exercise price less than the FMV on the date of grant (a "discounted option") may be subject to IRC §409A. Both types of options have their own reporting requirements.

- **Phantom Stock Plans**. Phantom stock is an arrangement under which deferred amounts are determined by reference to hypothetical "phantom" shares of the employer's stock without ever issuing the actual shares to the employee. The employee generally only receives the growth in the value of the share between the grant and exercise dates. Alternatively, the employee may be entitled to receive the entire value of the stock as well as any dividends paid from the time the employer grants the phantom shares. The employee may be paid in either stock or cash. The IRS notes that phantom stock plans are classified as Non-Qualified Deferred Compensation arrangements, not stock arrangements.

- **Stock Appreciation Rights**. A Stock Appreciation Right is an arrangement in which the employee is entitled only to the appreciation of the underlying stock between the issue and exercise dates. Because the employee only receives the appreciation, taxes are not due until the rights are exercised. When the right is exercised, the employee recognizes income and the employer recognizes an expense.

- **Restricted Stock Units**. Restricted stock units are agreements to pay either cash or stock at a specified date. One restricted stock unit typically represents one share of actual stock. Restricted stock units are not considered property for purposes of IRC §83 since no actual property has been transferred, and therefore an IRC §83(b) election cannot be made with respect to the grant of a restricted stock unit. Restricted stock units can be settled in either cash or stock.

- **Stock Warrants**. Stock warrants are similar to stock options and allow the holder to purchase a specified number of shares at a specified price and at a specified time. Stock warrants are often granted to non-employees and typically have longer terms than regular stock options. Unlike many other types of stock compensation, stock warrants may be transferred to other parties. Warrants may be taxable under IRC §83(b) subject to certain conditions.

Stock Transfer Considerations

With respect to stock transfers and potential tax consequences, the IRS guide notes six areas of focus for examiners, which we have briefly summarized below.

- **Whether the stock was actually transferred or not**. The IRS only considers stock to be transferred if the recipient has the risks and benefits of being an owner. Restrictions on sale of the stock, lack of voting, inability to participate in liquidating distributions, and the lack of rights to gains or losses on the stock could affect the status of the transfer.

- **Stock option transfers to a related person**. Transfer of compensatory stock options to a related person is a "listed transaction" as defined by the IRS and may require additional documentation and review procedures.

- **Whether there has been a reduction in the purchase price of a note used to acquire employer stock**. Promissory notes are sometimes issued in order to facilitate the purchase of stock. If the market price of the stock declines and the employer reduces the balance of the note in satisfaction of the exercise price of an option, various additional taxes may be triggered.

- **Whether a "substantial risk" of forfeiture exists**. Because risk of forfeiture typically only exists if transferred property rights are conditional upon future performance, the IRS does not consider property to be transferred if there is a substantial risk of forfeiture. In such cases, the compensation can only be recognized when the substantial risk of forfeiture has passed.

- **Whether dividends from restricted stock are received**. The receipt of dividends from substantially non-vested restricted stock is treated as additional compensation to the individual. Once the restricted stock award is vested, all dividends are treated as dividend income. However, with an §83(b) election, the income may be treated as dividend income rather than compensation.

- **Whether a Section 83(b) election has occurred**. An election pursuant to IRC §83(b) allows a recipient of restricted property to be taxed when the property is transferred instead of when the property actually vests (at a later date when the value may be higher). The IRS Guide outlines some of the restrictions relating to Section 83(b) elections and under what conditions the elections may be used. Sometimes Section 83(b) elections can have unintended consequences.

Conclusion

Obviously, every equity compensation plan is different and the particular tax treatment of a given security depends on the facts and circumstances of the arrangement. That said, the IRS guide provides a useful framework for understanding the general types of equity-based compensation and illustrates how an IRS examiner might approach an audit or review where equity-based compensation is a significant factor.

35

Look Before You Leap: Evaluating a Section 83(b) Election

Sujan Rajbhandary, CFA
Originally Published on September 4, 2015

Economic troubles in a faraway land and an agitating stock market closer to home appear to have precipitated a gloomier outlook for the funding prospects of young companies (technology startups). Whether or not the mood persists in the coming months, these times remind us that potential future states of the world include scenarios with less-than-spectacular results. Time, then, to spend a few minutes thinking about a choice that purports to deliver substantial tax savings to startup employees.[1]

An IRC Section 83(b) election allows an employee receiving equity compensation in the form of restricted stock to pay income taxes based on the fair market value of the award at the grant date. Increases in stock prices subsequent to the grant date are taxed at capital gains rates. If such an election is not made, the fair market value of the award is taxable at the higher ordinary income rates when and if the restricted shares vest. Critically, taxes paid pursuant to an 83(b) election will not be refundable in the future even if (a portion of) the awards do not vest, or if the shares turn out to be worthless.

It is easy to see how employees receiving restricted shares and making a Section 83(b) election can benefit if the price of the stock rises between the grant and vesting dates. An 83(b) election may appear especially appealing to (early stage) startup employees who tend to be (preter) naturally optimistic about the prospects of their employer companies. However, the benefits of a Section 83(b) election – especially after consideration of the risks involved – may be less significant than originally anticipated. Three conditions (often outside the control of the employees) must be met for an 83(b) election to provide a (risk-adjusted) advantage:

1. Securities awarded as compensation have relatively low values at the time of grant.

2. The exit event for the employer company, or other transactions that may provide liquidity to the employees, occurs at relatively high implied valuations.

3. Employees remain employed at the granting company until the awards vest.

This analysis will primarily address the first condition.

An Example

A common misconception is that shares awarded as compensation have minimal (if any) value at the grant date and thus, the underlying stock price has nowhere to go but up. In our experience, employees too often make the 83(b) election under the assumption that the fair market value of the stock is at or near $0 per share at the grant date. A fictitious example can perhaps illustrate why this may be a faulty assumption in the face of a contemporaneous funding round (or transactions involving common shares or other securities of the company).

A couple of entrepreneurs found Company A at Date 0, and proceed to introduce a disruptive technology and begin to achieve some market traction. At a subsequent Date 1, Company A raises $19 million in equity by issuing 950,000 Series X Preferred shares at $20 per share. A VC firm and the founders participate in the Series X Round. Concurrently, Company A also issues 50,000 Common shares as equity compensation to its employees in the form of restricted shares.

The Series X Preferred shares have the following rights and downside protections:

*   **Liquidation preferences** equal to 1.2x invested capital ($22.8 million). The liquidation preference would not be available in the case of an IPO exit.

- **Conversion rights** to exchange the Series X Preferred for Common shares at $20 per share.

Assume that the investment decision at Date 1 was predicated on three exit scenarios for Company A at Date 2, four years after the funding.

- An IPO to sell (new) 250,000 Common shares at $80 per share. Series X Preferred shares convert to Common immediately preceding the IPO. Based on the IPO price, the aggregate value of the Series X shares is $76 million, while the employees' stock will be worth $4 million.

Figure 35.1

	Date 0 (Founding)	Date 1 (Funding)	Date 2 - Alt 1 (Exit - IPO)	Date 2 - Alt 2 (Exit - Strategic)	Date 2 - Alt 3 (Exit - Fire Sale)
Share Count					
Series X	10	950,000	950,000	950,000	950,000
Common - Employees	0	50,000	50,000	50,000	50,000
Common - New Investors at IPO	na	na	250,000	0	0
Total Number of Shares	10	1,000,000	1,250,000	1,000,000	1,000,000
Valuation					
Per Share Price		$20.00	$80.00	$80.00	$22.54
Enterprise Value at Exit		na	$100,000,000	$80,000,000	$22,540,000
Exit Waterfall to Various Classes					
Do Preferred Shares Convert?			Yes	Yes	No
Series X			$76,000,000	$76,000,000	$22,540,000
Common - Employees			$4,000,000	$4,000,000	$0
Common - New Investors at IPO			$20,000,000	$0	$0
Total Proceeds			$100,000,000	$80,000,000	$22,540,000

Market Participant Perspectives

Figure 35.2

	Date 0 (Founding)	Date 1 (Funding)	Date 2 - Alt 1 (Exit - IPO)	Date 2 - Alt 2 (Exit - Strategic)	Date 2 - Alt 3 (Exit - Fire Sale)
Exit Waterfall to Various Classes					
Series X			$76,000,000	$76,000,000	$22,540,000
Exit Probabilities			10.0%	10.0%	80.0%
Series X					
Expected Future Value	$33,232,000				
Holding Period	4				
Discount Rate	15%				
Present Value	$19,000,504				
Per Share	$20.00				

Figure 35.3

	Date 0 (Founding)	Date 1 (Funding)	Date 2 - Alt 1 (Exit - IPO)	Date 2 - Alt 2 (Exit - Strategic)	Date 2 - Alt 3 (Exit - Fire Sale)
Exit Waterfall to Various Classes					
Series X			$4,000,000	$4,000,000	$0
Exit Probabilities			10.0%	10.0%	80.0%
Employee Compensation					
Expected Future Value	$800,000				
Holding Period	4				
Discount Rate	20%				
Present Value	$385,802				
Per Share	$7.72				
As % of Series X	38.6%				

- A strategic sale of Company A for $80 million. Again, Series X Preferred shares convert to Common and collect $76 million. Common shareholders (employees) receive the balance (or $4 million) of the exit proceeds.

- A fire sale of the Company for $22.5 million, such that the entirety of the proceeds is used to satisfy the liquidation preferences of the Series X Preferred shares. The common shareholders (employees) receive nothing.

Let us further assume that a rate of return (discount rate) of 15% is consistent with Series X investor expectations. Given the holding period of 4 years, assigned probabilities of 10% for the IPO exit, 10% for the strategic sale, and 80% for the fire sale scenario reconcile to the Series X Preferred price at Date 1 ($20 per share).[2]

The foregoing outlines a barebones framework around the investment decision. The assumptions used within this framework are almost sufficient to derive an implied price for the Common shares granted as employee compensation. In light of the rate of return for the Series X investors, let us assume that a reasonable discount rate for the common shares is 20%. The same framework we used to examine the Series X investment price implies a price of $7.72 per Common share (or approximately 39% of the price of Series X Preferred per share).[3]

What is Reasonable?

We stress that 39% is only an illustrative figure, which is the result of the simple assumptions we make regarding capital structure and exit prospects of a fictitious company. The objective of the example is to simply illustrate that given expectations of potentially successful exits for the company, it is reasonable to conclude a value of greater than $0 per Common share.

Actual values of Common shares relative to Preferred will vary based on the length of the expected holding period, exit scenarios (price and likelihood), rights and protections accorded to the Preferred, potential dilution from future funding rounds, appropriate discount rates, DLOMs, and other factors. To simplify considerably, the values of the various securities in the capital stack represent a zero-sum carve-out of the enterprise value. Accordingly, more rights and protections accorded to the Preferred shares results in a relatively lower value conclusion for the Common shares. For instance, all else equal, if the Series X

Preferred in our example also had participation rights (no cap), the value of the Common would decrease to $6.62 per share before the application of DLOM. Assuming a 20% DLOM would suggest a value of $5.29 per share (or approximately 26% of the price per Series X Preferred share).

As the foregoing example shows, economic logic suggests that it may be unreasonable to expect shares awarded as compensation to have minimal value at the grant date, especially if there are contemporaneous funding or transaction activities. Valuation best practices codified in the AICPA *Accounting & Valuation Guide Valuation of Privately-Held-Company Equity Securities Issued as Compensation* confirm the necessity of using a valuation approach that recognizes the value accruing to common shares attributable to the right to participate in successful exits. As a result, potential appreciation of the shares between the grant and vest dates may be more limited than is commonly believed.

Other Conditions

The second condition necessary for a Section 83(b) election to be beneficial to employees concerns the exit price commanded by the employer company (or, the Common shares if secondary avenues to liquidity are available). This condition relates to the risk inherent in making an 83(b) election for employees of early-stage companies. The exit potential of an employer company may depend on many more factors than just the effort put forth by the employees (not a comprehensive list):

- Technical viability of the product or service the company is pursuing.

- Market acceptance of the product or service.

- Competitive forces.

- Prudent management.

- Market perception of the industry within which the company operates.

- Prospects of the broader (even global) economy.

- Relative over-valuation in prior funding rounds.

Finally, the third condition necessary for a Section 83(b) election to be beneficial to employees relates to the likelihood of continued employment at the granting company. While any number of circumstances could lead to early termination of employment at the company that grants stock compensation, an 83(b) election usually represents a wrong-way bet on the part of the employees. Early termination from a job (for whatever reason) results in a double economic hit – 1) forfeiture of unvested shares, and 2) inability to recoup taxes already paid taxes for unvested shares. All this at a time when the employee could probably least afford economic hits in the first place.

Conclusion

To summarize:

- It is not reasonable to assume that Common shares in early stage (or late stage, for that matter) companies are near-worthless. Following best practices (and economic logic), even out-of-the-money equity awards will have value in accord with the holder's right to participate in future successful exists, should they occur.

- If prospects of the employer company sour after an 83(b) election, employees will have already paid (certain) taxes based on a higher value for a security that is now less valuable than at the grant date (and vesting may yet be uncertain).

Nothing in this post is intended to be legal or tax advice, but we hope all employees facing the prospect of a Section 83(b) election will make well-considered choices.

End Notes

[1] We are not tax experts. Those interested in specific guidance for tax or legal matters should seek competent professional advice.

[2] {10%, 10%, 80%} is just one of many possible assumption sets that reconciles to $20 per Series X Preferred share.

[3] The price of $7.72 per share is before the application of any discount for lack of marketability (DLOM), which is almost always a valid consideration for Common shares. For example, if the appropriate DLOM were 20%, the conclusion of value would be $6.17 per Common share (or approximately 31% of the price per Series X Preferred share). We will address DLOMs within the context of valuing various securities that make up the capital stack of young companies in a future blog post.

36

A Layperson's Guide to the OPM: Everything You Always Wanted to Know About the OPM, But Were Afraid to Ask

Travis W. Harms, CFA, CPA/ABV
Originally Published on May 16, 2016

The option pricing model, or OPM, is one of the shiniest new tools in the valuation specialist's toolkit. While specialists have grown accustomed to working with the tool and have faith in the results of its use, many non-specialists remain wary, as the model – and its typical presentation – has all the trappings of a proverbial black box. The purpose of this post is to clarify the fundamental insight underlying the model and illustrate its application so that non-specialist users of valuation reports can gain greater comfort with the and to address some qualitative concerns regarding use of the method in practice.

What is the OPM Used For?

First, a bit of ground-clearing. What does the OPM not do? The OPM is not a method for determining the value of a business enterprise. The method does not consider the value of the subject business enterprise's assets and liabilities, evaluate the present value of projected cash flows, or concern itself with a comparison of the subject business enterprise to similar businesses with observable market values.

The OPM becomes useful only after the value of the business enterprise has been determined through application of valuation methods under the asset-based, income and market approaches. The OPM is a tool for allocating the total equity value to individual ownership classes in a complex capital structure. For enterprises with a simple capital structure (i.e., a single class of common equity), the OPM is not necessary and should not be used. However, when the subject business enterprise features multiple classes of preferred and/or common equity with differing economic rights, the OPM can be a most effective tool for differentiating the value of the various ownership classes. Such complex capital structures are most frequently encountered in early-stage enterprises, which are frequently valued for equity compensation and portfolio fair value reporting.

What is the Fundamental Insight Underlying the OPM?

The "Eureka!" moment behind the OPM is the recognition that the payoffs to complex securities with arcane features can be mimicked through an appropriately-constructed portfolio of component securities (most commonly fractional call options or digital options with varying strike prices). As a result, what may seem on the surface to be an impossible valuation task can be mastered if the economic payoffs for a complex security are untangled and re-cast as a bundle of simple securities that can be more readily valued. The method holds out the promise of replacing subjective judgment with replicable analysis. Hence, the esteem in which the method is held among auditors.

Consider a simple example. SimpleCo is capitalized with a single class of preferred shares and a single class of common shares. Upon liquidation or sale of SimpleCo, the preferred shareholders are entitled to receive $500, with the residual accruing to the common shareholders. The economic terms of the capital structure are summarized in Figure 36.1.

Two observations can be made from a brief study of Figure 36.1.

1. **Financial engineering does not create value**. In every possible state of the world, the sum of the payoffs to the preferred and common shareholders is equal to the equity value. Creative pie-slicing does not make the pie any bigger.

2. **The payoffs to the common shareholders have the same basic shape as a call option**. The holder of a call option receives no payoff when the stock price is less than or equal to the strike price. However, the call

Figure 36.1

Enterprise Value	Preferred Shareholders	Common Shareholders
$0	$0	$0
$100	$100	$0
$200	$200	$0
$300	$300	$0
$400	$400	$0
$500	$500	$0
$600	$500	$100
$700	$500	$200
$800	$500	$300
$900	$500	$400
$1,000	$500	$500

Figure 36.2

Enterprise Value	=	Preferred Shareholders	+	Common Shareholders
EV	=	(EV - $500 Call)	+	$500 Call

option holder participates dollar-for-dollar in appreciation above the strike price.

In light of these observations, we can express the value of the preferred and common share as shown in Figure 36.2.

By recasting the preferred and common equity classes into the component securities, the subjective judgment associated with selecting the appropriate yield on the preferred shares has been eliminated, as the value of the preferred shares is simply the excess of equity value over the value of a call option with a strike price of $500.

Figure 36.3: Capital Structure - ComplexCo

	Liquidation Preference	Liquidation Priority	Conversion/ Exercise Price	Fully- Diluted Shares	% of Total
Class A Preferred	$1,000	Pari Passu	$2.00	500	19.6%
Class B Preferred	1,500	Pari Passu	$5.00	300	11.8%
Common Shares	0	Residual	na	1,500	58.8%
Warrants	0	Residual	$10.00	250	9.8%
Total	$2,500			2,550	100.0%

What is a "Breakpoint"?

Moving to a more complex example will allow us to explain and define additional vocabulary terms from the OPM. Figure 36.3 summarizes the capital structure for ComplexCo.

While this capital structure is still quite tame relative to many real-world counterparts, it is sufficiently complex to illustrate the fundamental tools used in OPM applications.

One could construct a payoff table similar to that in Figure 36.1. While certainly possible, doing so can become a bit cumbersome as the complexity of the capital structure increases. As a shortcut, valuation specialists identify the relevant "breakpoints" in the capital structure. In the OPM, a breakpoint is an equity value beyond which the marginal allocation of incremental value to the various equity classes changes. SimpleCo had a single breakpoint, while ComplexCo will prove to have four. We often see cases in which a dozen or more can be identified.

Breakpoints are identified starting with an equity value of $0. For ComplexCo, the Class A and Class B preferred shares participate on a *pari passu* basis, so the first breakpoint is the aggregate liquidation preference, or $2,500 (the total "Net Proceeds" in Figure 36.4). Additional elements of Figure 36.4 will be explained as we proceed through the example.

For equity values from $0 to $2,500, the Class A preferred shareholders will receive 40% of value, and the Class B preferred shareholders will receive 60%.

For equity values above $2,500, the marginal proceeds will be allocated differently, as shown in Figure 36.5. This change in allocation is what makes $2,500 a breakpoint in this example.

The next change in the allocation of proceeds will occur when the Class A Preferred shares convert to common. At common share values greater than $2.00 per share, the Class A Preferred shareholders will elect to convert, as their net proceeds from conversion will exceed the liquidation preference. As a result,

Figure 36.4: Breakpoint #1 - Class A & Class B Liquidation Preference

	Shares	Gross Proceeds	Exercise Price	Net Proceeds	% of Total	Marginal Proceeds	% of Total
Preference Claims							
Class A Preferred		$1,000	na	$1,000	40.0%	$1,000	40.0%
Class B Preferred		1,500	na	1,500	60.0%	1,500	60.0%
As-If Converted Shares	$0.00						
Class A Preferred	0	0	na	0	0.0%	0	0.0%
Class B Preferred	0	0	na	0	0.0%	0	0.0%
Common Shares	1,500	0	na	0	0.0%	0	0.0%
Warrants	0	0	0	0	0.0%	0	0.0%
Total	1,500	$2,500	$0	$2,500	100.0%	$2,500	100.0%

Figure 36.5: Breakpoint #2 - Class A Converts to Common

	Shares	Gross Proceeds	Exercise Price	Net Proceeds	% of Total	Marginal Proceeds	% of Total
Preference Claims							
Class A Preferred		$0	na	$0	0.0%	($1,000)	-33.3%
Class B Preferred		1,500	na	1,500	27.3%	0	0.0%
As-If Converted Shares	$2.00						
Class A Preferred	500	1,000	na	1,000	18.2%	1,000	33.3%
Class B Preferred	0	0	na	0	0.0%	0	0.0%
Common Shares	1,500	3,000	na	3,000	54.5%	3,000	100.0%
Warrants	0	0	0	0	0.0%	0	0.0%
Total	2,000	$5,500	$0	$5,500	100.0%	$3,000	100.0%

the number of as-if converted shares increases, but the liquidation preference attributable to the Class A shares is forfeited. The corresponding breakpoint equity value is $5,500.

Breakpoint #3 corresponds to the common share price that will induce the Class B Preferred shareholders to convert to common shares ($5.00). In other words, the Class B Preferred shareholders will elect to convert, and be treated as common shareholders when the total equity value exceeds $11,500.

Figure 36.6: Breakpoint #3 – Class B Converts to Common

	Shares	Gross Proceeds	Exercise Price	Net Proceeds	% of Total	Marginal Proceeds	% of Total
Preference Claims							
Class A Preferred		$0	na	$0	0.0%	$0	0.0%
Class B Preferred		0	na	0	0.0%	(1,500)	-25.0%
As-If Converted Shares	**$5.00**						
Class A Preferred	500	2,500	na	2,500	21.7%	1,500	25.0%
Class B Preferred	300	1,500	na	1,500	13.0%	1,500	25.0%
Common Shares	1,500	7,500	na	7,500	65.2%	4,500	75.0%
Warrants	0	0	0	0	0.0%	0	0.0%
Total	2,300	$11,500	$0	$11,500	100.0%	$6,000	100.0%

Figure 36.7: Breakpoint #4 – Warrants Exercise

	Shares	Gross Proceeds	Exercise Price	Net Proceeds	% of Total	Marginal Proceeds	% of Total
Preference Claims							
Class A Preferred		$0	na	$0	0.0%	$0	0.0%
Class B Preferred		0	na	0	0.0%	0	0.0%
As-If Converted Shares	**$10.00**						
Class A Preferred	500	5,000	na	5,000	21.7%	2,500	21.7%
Class B Preferred	300	3,000	na	3,000	13.0%	1,500	13.0%
Common Shares	1,500	15,000	na	15,000	65.2%	7,500	65.2%
Warrants	250	2,500	(2,500)	0	0.0%	0	0.0%
Total	2,550	$25,500	($2,500)	$23,000	100.0%	$11,500	100.0%

As shown in Figure 36.7, Breakpoint #4 corresponds to the exercise of outstanding warrants. Note that while the warrants will be exercised at $10.00 per share, the warrant holders will pay $10.00 per share to do so, so the net proceeds to the warrants remains $0 at that point, and the equity value breakpoint is the total "Net Proceeds".

Beyond the last breakpoint, marginal proceeds can be allocated according to an additional illustrative payoff schedule assuming some arbitrary share price in excess of the last breakpoint, as shown in Figure 36.8.

What is a "Tranche"?

The next step in applying the OPM is to build a matrix that identifies the marginal allocation percentages between the various breakpoints. For purposes of the OPM, a "tranche" is the difference between two adjacent breakpoints. The marginal proceeds within a given tranche are allocated to the various equity classes in fixed proportions.

The marginal tranche allocation matrix summarizes the relative allocation to the various equity classes within the respective tranches. The allocations were calculated in the corresponding breakpoint tables. The illustrative upside scenario (Figure 36.8) allows us to confirm marginal allocation percentages for values in excess of the final breakpoint. Note that the marginal allocation

Figure 36.8: Illustrative Upside

	Shares	Gross Proceeds	Exercise Price	Net Proceeds	% of Total	Marginal Proceeds	% of Total
Preference Claims							
Class A Preferred		$0	na	$0	0.0%	$0	0.0%
Class B Preferred		0	na	0	0.0%	0	0.0%
As-If Converted Shares	$15.00						
Class A Preferred	500	7,500	na	7,500	21.0%	2,500	19.6%
Class B Preferred	300	4,500	na	4,500	12.6%	1,500	11.8%
Common Shares	1,500	22,500	na	22,500	62.9%	7,500	58.8%
Warrants	250	3,750	(2,500)	1,250	3.5%	1,250	9.8%
Total	2,550	$38,250	($2,500)	$35,750	100.0%	$12,750	100.0%

percentages for the final tranche are equal to the proportion of total fully-diluted shares outstanding from each equity class.

The next step is to determine the value of each tranche. In doing so, we will work from right to left. Recall from our SimpleCo example that the portion of equity value in excess of a given amount can be calculated with reference to a call option on the underlying equity value with a corresponding strike price. In the case of ComplexCo, the value of the upside in excess of the final breakpoint ($23,000) is equal to the value of a call option having a strike price equal to that breakpoint value.

What about the value of the next tranche down? Following the same approach, the value of all of the upside beyond $11,500 is equal to the value of a call option on the underlying equity value having that strike price. The value of this call option represents the combined value of Tranche D and Tranche E. Since the value of Tranche E is known, the value of Tranche D can readily be calculated by subtraction. As shown in Figure 36.10, the value of lower tranches is measured following the same procedure. Note that – in keeping with first observation above – the sum of the individual tranche values is equal to the equity value. Financial engineering can create complexity, but does not create value.

Finally, the tranche values are apportioned to the individual equity classes in accordance with the percentages from the marginal tranche allocation matrix

Figure 36.9: Marginal Tranche Allocation Matrix

	Tranche A	Tranche B	Tranche C	Tranche D	Tranche E
Upper Breakpoint	$2,500	$5,500	$11,500	$23,000	$35,750
Lower Breakpoint	$0	$2,500	$5,500	$11,500	$23,000
Tranche Width	$2,500	$3,000	$6,000	$11,500	$12,750
Marginal Allocations					
Class A Preferred	40.0%	0.0%	25.0%	21.7%	19.6%
Class B Preferred	60.0%	0.0%	0.0%	13.0%	11.8%
Common Shares	0.0%	100.0%	75.0%	65.2%	58.8%
Warrants	0.0%	0.0%	0.0%	0.0%	9.8%

% of Marginal Proceeds from Breakpoint payoff tables

(Figure 36.9). As shown in Figure 36.11, the value of a particular equity class
is the sum of the values of that class's respective allocations for each tranche.

Figure 36.10: Derivation of Tranche Values

	Tranche A	Tranche B	Tranche C	Tranche D	Tranche E
Stock price (S)	$17,500	$17,500	$17,500	$17,500	$17,500
Exercise price (K)	$0	$2,500	$5,500	$11,500	$23,000
Time to expiration (T)	4.0	4.0	4.0	4.0	4.0
Volatility (σ)	35.0%	35.0%	35.0%	35.0%	35.0%
Risk-free rate (r)	1.500%	1.500%	1.500%	1.500%	1.500%
Value of call options	$17,500	$15,148	$12,426	$8,033	$3,514
Tranche Values	$2,352	$2,722	$4,393	$4,519	$3,514

Calculated by subtraction

Figure 36.11: Calculation of Equity Class Values

		Tranche A	Tranche B	Tranche C	Tranche D	Tranche E	Total
Tranche Values	A	$2,352	$2,722	$4,393	$4,519	$3,514	$17,500
Marginal Allocations							
Class A Preferred	B	40.0%	0.0%	25.0%	21.7%	19.6%	
Class B Preferred		60.0%	0.0%	0.0%	13.0%	11.8%	
Common Shares		0.0%	100.0%	75.0%	65.2%	58.8%	
Warrants		0.0%	0.0%	0.0%	0.0%	9.8%	
Marginal Values							
Class A Preferred	A x B	941	0	1,098	982	689	3,710
Class B Preferred		1,411	0	0	589	413	2,414
Common Shares		0	2,722	3,295	2,947	2,067	11,031
Warrants		0	0	0	0	344	344
Total		$2,352	$2,722	$4,393	$4,519	$3,514	$17,500

Calculated by addition

The aggregate values are converted to per share amounts in Figure 36.12.

On a per share basis, the results conform to expectations regarding the relative value of the various classes. The higher liquidation preference of the Class B preferred shares causes those shares to be most valuable. The common shares, which do not have any liquidation preference, are worth less than either class of preferred shares. Finally, the strike price on the warrants reduces the value of those instruments relative to common shares.

Other Economic Features That Can Be Modeled in OPM

The ComplexCo example included the most common economic rights (liquidation preferences, conversion features, exercise prices) found in equity instruments. The OPM can also accommodate dividends, to the extent they accumulate and affect liquidation preferences and/or conversion. Participation rights for preferred shares allow preferred shareholders to receive – in addition to their base liquidation preference – additional proceeds at liquidation on an as-if-converted basis, often up to some cap, expressed as a multiple of the liquidation preference. The mechanics of participation rights can vary modestly, but in any event can be directly modeled within the OPM framework.

More exotic, and less common, features of preferred shares include price or return hurdles that influence the allocation of proceeds to the equity holders. The OPM can also be accommodated to these features. So long, as the feature can be reduced to a function of total equity value (i.e., for a given total equity value, there is one and only one possible allocation of proceeds to the various classes), the feature can be valued within the OPM framework.

Figure 36.12: Calculation of Per Share Values

	Total Value	Fully-Diluted Shares	Value per Share
Class A Preferred	$3,710	500	$7.42
Class B Preferred	$2,414	300	$8.05
Common Shares	$11,031	1,500	$7.35
Warrants	$344	250	$1.38

Not all features can be reduced to a function of total equity value, however. The OPM cannot be adapted to directly value differential voting rights, price protection or ratchet provisions, drag-along and tag-along rights, and pre-emptive rights. Some notable recent late-stage rounds have featured complex anti-dilution provisions, including guaranteed minimum returns in the event of an IPO that go beyond the protections offered by traditional price ratchets. When such features are present, valuation specialists need to consider whether a discrete adjustment to the results of the OPM analysis should be made in measuring fair value.

The OPM allocates the value of the existing capital structure, with the volatility parameter determining the potential changes in the value of the existing equity classes. Future issuances of additional equity are assumed to pull their own economic weight (i.e., neither contribute to, nor detract from, the value of the existing equity classes). As a result, there is no need to make assumptions in the OPM for the amount, timing, or pricing of future equity raises.

Assessing Reasonableness: Inputs

Beyond the formal elements of the capital structure that define breakpoints and tranche allocations, the required inputs to the OPM are the traditional Black-Scholes parameters. Figure 36.10 displayed the inputs used to allocate the value of ComplexCo.

The OPM inputs can be developed, and tested for reasonableness, in the same manner as in applications of the Black-Scholes model.

- **Stock Price**. The stock price in the OPM is the total equity value of the subject business. The total equity value is derived through application of the traditional valuation methods under the asset-based, income and market approaches. As will be discussed in a subsequent section of this post, a known value for a particular component of the capital structure can be used to find the implied total equity value (the "backsolve" method).

- **Exercise Price**. The exercise prices in the OPM correspond to the equity value breakpoints identified in the formal analysis of the capital structure.

- **Time to Expiration**. In applying the OPM, one must assume a single point estimate for when liquidity will be achieved, either through dissolution, strategic sale, or IPO. While the actual time to expiration cannot be known with certainty, reasonable estimates can generally be made by reference to the subject company's life cycle stage, funding needs, and strategic outlook.

- **Volatility**. As with time to expiration, volatility cannot be directly observed. The most common starting point for volatility analysis is an examination of historical return volatility for a group of peer public companies. If reliable data is available, implied volatility from publicly traded options on the shares of such companies may also be consulted. Analysts adjust the observed peer volatility measures to take into account life cycle stage, remaining milestones, and other qualitative factors pertaining to the subject company.

- **Risk-free Rate**. The risk-free rate corresponds to the assumed time to expiration.

The most challenging assumptions to establish and support in application of the OPM are the time to expiration and volatility. As discussed in the following section, testing the sensitivity of the OPM output to variation in these inputs is a critical element of assessing reasonableness.

Assessing Reasonableness: Output

We assessed the reasonableness of the OPM output from one perspective earlier in this post. Report reviewers can quickly confirm the most basic mechanical integrity of an OPM through three easy preliminary checks: (1) the sum of the aggregate equity class allocations equals the total equity value of the subject company, (2) the sum of the fully-diluted shares used to calculate value per share equals that in the capitalization table, and (3) the rank order of the per share value conclusions is consistent with the liquidity preferences, conversion rights, and exercise prices pertinent to the various equity classes. These simple checks will not uncover all potential modelling errors, but they do eliminate a good portion of the most egregious potential pitfalls.

Beyond mere mechanical integrity, an additional step in assessing the reasonableness of the OPM output is to consider the sensitivity of the resulting allocation to changes in key inputs, principally time to expiration and volatility. Figure 36.13 provides such sensitivity analysis for ComplexCo.

We can make a few general observations from the sensitivity analysis in Figure 36.13.

1. Since the OPM is an allocation model, the total value of the equity classes is unaffected by changes in inputs. The only impact such changes can have is on the relative allocation to various classes. This is purely a zero-sum game; for one class to increase in value, one or more other classes must decrease in value.

2. The sensitivity results are easiest to interpret for the warrants. As the junior-most security in the capital structure, the sensitivity to changes in OPM inputs is unambiguous. Increases in time to expiration cause the allocation to warrants to increase, as do increases in volatility. Furthermore, because the warrants are at the bottom of the capital stack,

Figure 36.13: Sensitivity to OPM Inputs

| | Volatility = 35% | | | Time to Expiration = 4 yrs | | |
| | Changes in Time to Expiration | | | Changes in Volatility | | |
	2 yrs	4 yrs	6 yrs	20%	35%	50%
Total Value						
Class A Preferred	$3,744	$3,710	$3,696	$3,764	$3,710	$3,698
Class B Preferred	2,345	2,414	2,458	2,304	2,414	2,526
Common Shares	11,221	11,031	10,878	11,290	11,031	10,729
Warrants	189	344	467	142	344	546
Total	$17,500	$17,500	$17,500	$17,500	$17,500	$17,500
Per Share Value						
Class A Preferred	$7.49	$7.42	$7.39	$7.53	$7.42	$7.40
Class B Preferred	$7.82	$8.05	$8.19	$7.68	$8.05	$8.42
Common Shares	$7.48	$7.35	$7.25	$7.53	$7.35	$7.15
Warrants	$0.76	$1.38	$1.87	$0.57	$1.38	$2.19
Diff b/t Class B & Common	*$0.34*	*$0.69*	*$0.94*	*$0.15*	*$0.69*	*$1.27*

the sensitivity of value to changes in inputs is magnified relative to other equity classes.

3.   The Class B preferred shares benefit from downside protection, as the proximity of the conversion price ($5.00) to the current common share price increases the likelihood that the liquidation preference will preserve returns to the Class B preferred shareholders. The payoff to the Class B preferred shareholders is asymmetric since the upside is unlimited through the conversion feature, while the downside is constrained by the liquidation preference. As a result, assumptions that increase the dispersion of potential future outcomes (longer time to expiration and higher volatility) cause the value of the Class B preferred shares to increase.

4.   The junior preferred shares (Class A) are directionally aligned with the common shares, although the fixed liquidation preference dampens volatility relative to the common shares. In cases of short times to expiration and low volatility, the per share value for Class A approaches that of the common as the likelihood that the current share price ($7.35) will fall below the Class A conversion price ($2.00) diminishes to a trivial level.

5.   The sensitivity of the common shares, which are situated between the preferred classes and the warrants, is less predictable. In this case, the warrants have a parasitic relationship to the common shares, such that increases in the value of the warrants are accompanied by decreases in common share value. This relationship does not always obtain, however; the relative proportions of the instruments in the capital structure and the "moneyness" of the various capital structure components will determine the sensitivity of the common.

With reference to seniority, the equity classes at the "edges" of the capital structure are those that experience the greatest relative benefit from a skewed outcome. The most senior class benefits (on a relative basis) from the liquidation preference in a downside scenario, while the most junior class experiences the greatest marginal benefit from an upside scenario. Since the classes at the "edges" gain the most from skewed outcomes, they exhibit the greatest sensitivity to volatility and time factors, with the "interior" classes are less sensitive.

Figure 36.14: Seniority and Sensitivity to Volatility

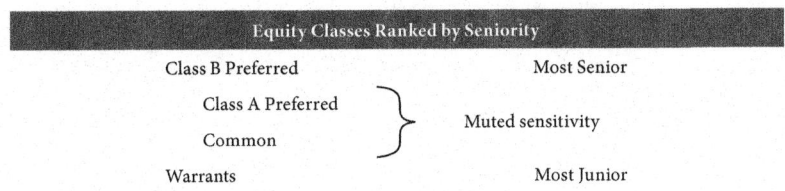

Strengths and Weaknesses Relative to PWERM

The primary analytical alternative to the OPM is the probability-weighted expected return method, or PWERM as it is affectionately known. Whereas the OPM is a continuous model, with potential future outcomes assumed to occur pursuant to a lognormal distribution, the PWERM is a discrete model which considers a finite number of analyst-selected potential outcomes and associated probabilities. In contrast to the OPM, the PWERM pulls double duty as both a valuation method and a means of simultaneously allocating the resulting value to the various equity classes.

Figure 36.15 summarizes a comparison of the two models along a variety of axes.

Reliability of Backsolve Application of OPM

The OPM is not a valuation method. However, if the value of any component of the capital structure is known – through either a contemporaneous primary issuance or secondary trade – the enterprise value corresponding to that value can be determined. Using the OPM to work backward from output to an indication of implied total equity value is known as the "backsolve" method.

As an example, consider the case of ComplexCo at the time the Class B preferred shares were issued at a price of $5.00 per share (one year prior to the valuation date in our Part 1 example). What was the implied total equity value of the company at that time? By starting with the known value of $5.00 per Class B preferred share, we can work backward, developing estimates for all the other assumptions, to determine the implied total equity value. In this case, we conclude that all assumptions are unchanged from Figure 36.10, with the exception

Figure 36.15: Comparison of OPM and PWERM

	OPM	PWERM
Required Assumptions	In addition to the breakpoints and tranche allocations dictated by the capital structure terms, requires only five inputs.	Requires more assumptions than the OPM. Analyst must specify amount, timing and probability of future liquidity events as well as dilution from future financing rounds and class-specific discount rates.
Sensitivity to Assumptions	As shown in Figure 36.13, sensitivity for many classes is somewhat muted. Since the OPM is only an allocation method, the impact of changes in inputs on allocation is generally tame compared to that in typical valuation methods.	Since the PWERM is both a valuation and allocation method, sensitivity to changes in inputs is potentially greater than with OPM.
Flexibility / Adaptability	Small number of required assumptions limits the flexibility and adaptability of the model. Cannot accommodate some common features of preferred shares such as mandatory conversion at IPO, IPO price guarantees and the like. The assumed lognormal distribution of outcomes may not be representative for many development-stage entities.	Can be readily adapted to unique features, such as price protection or ratchets. Offers the flexibility to consider a range of potential future outcomes that more closely represent the market participant perspective than a lognormal distribution. Allows the analyst to consider outcomes at different times, and to model dilution from future funding rounds (even down rounds).
Transparency	Host of intermediate calculations and lack of familiarity with breakpoint analysis on the part of many report users contribute to perception that method is a "black box".	Generally intuitive, allocation of proceeds for each discrete scenario is readily checked for conformity to governing documents.
Auditability	While not necessarily intuitive for non-specialists, small number of assumptions and translation of governing documents to formal structure of model is highly auditable.	While the required inputs correlate to assumptions that market participants actually make, convincing and documentable support for these estimates may prove elusive.

Figure 36.16: Backsolve Method Using the OPM

	Total Value	Fully-Diluted Shares	Value per Share
Class A Preferred	$1,618	500	$3.24
Class B Preferred	$1,500	300	**$5.00**
Common Shares	$4,089	1,500	$2.73
Warrants	$35	250	$0.14
Total	$7,242		

of time to expiration, which is five years, instead of four. As shown in Figure 36.16, the resulting total equity value is $7,242 at the issuance date, compared to $17,500 at the later valuation date from our prior example in Part 1 of this post.

This procedure is reasonable and appropriate in many circumstances. In our experience, however, it is important to keep in mind how the limitations of the OPM (primarily the lognormal distribution of outcomes) can distort the results of the analysis. When reading "backwards" from the value of a single equity class to the value of all equity, the effect of such distortions can be magnified. In our experience, the potential magnitude of such distortion is greatest when the known value is for the most senior security in the capital structure. In many cases, the lognormal assumption causes total loss scenarios to be under-represented in the probability distribution of potential future outcomes relative to market participant expectations. When combined with the use of the risk-free rate in a risk neutral framework, the OPM may assign greater value to the liquidation preference than market participants do. This can cause the difference between the most senior preferred class and other components of the capital structure to be exaggerated, resulting in an understated total equity value.

In our view, these distortions can be further aggravated when the equity class used to calibrate the total equity value accounts for only a small portion of the subject company's capital structure. In our practice, we temper the effect of this issue by also giving weight to the total equity value which is the product of the known per share price and the fully-diluted share count.

Reconciling the OPM with Market Participant Perspectives

There is an irony at the heart of fair value measurement. Fair value is, by definition, a market participant concept. In other words, a "correct" fair value measurement will reflect the exit price for the subject asset among a group of relevant market participants. However, some techniques for measuring fair value are rarely, if ever, used by actual market participants.

In our experience working with market participants in early-stage companies, new financing rounds are generally priced through a two-step process: (1) negotiate the pre-money total equity value of the company, and (2) divide that figure by the fully-diluted share count. These market participants clearly understand that the economic rights associated with senior preferred shares are valuable. However, they do not develop or express a discrete estimate of that value. We suspect that there are at least two potential explanations for this. First, the economic rights that benefit the senior preferred shares may be the required "sweetener" to arrive at the headline total equity value. Second, in many early-stage companies, the actual benefit of a liquidation preference may be perceived as limited. Certainly, the scenario that would trigger payout of a liquidation preference, in lieu of participating as common shareholder following conversion, is sub-optimal. If the most likely outcomes are smashing success (in which case everyone converts and is treated equally) or abysmal failure (in which case being first in line to get nothing is not helpful), market participants may be less impressed by the economic rights accruing to the senior securities than the OPM would seem to be.

Assuming we are right, this perfectly rational behavior on the part of market participants can put those with the responsibility to measure fair value in a difficult spot. Consider a company that recently closed a $20 million Class B round, with customary liquidation preferences and conversion rights. The term sheet states that the pre-money equity value is $100 million. There are 10 million Class A preferred and common shares outstanding, and the issuance price for the Class B round is $10 per share.

As shown in Figure 36.17, there are three logical possibilities in this case. The only case that is inconsistent with the OPM is the one that reflects the actual, stated terms of the transaction.

Figure 36.17: Reconciliation to Market Participant Perspective

TEV = $100 million	TEV = $100 million	TEV < $100 million
Class B > $10.00	Class B = $10.00 per Term Sheet	Class B = $10.00
Consistent with OPM	Not Consistent with OPM	Consistent with OPM

There is no simple solution to this conundrum. However, to our mind it does underscore the appropriate posture toward analytical tools like the OPM. The fair value measurement tool should serve the market participant perspective; the market participant perspective should not be subordinated to the fair value measurement tool, no matter how insightful and "correct" it may be. Fidelity reports identical per share values for different equity classes of a given investee company. In doing so, one is effectively disregarding the differential economic rights of the various classes. Strictly speaking, such a conclusion is economically untenable. Yet, it likely mirrors how Fidelity, and other market participants, actually view value.

Conclusion

Use of the OPM in fair value measurement is growing. The model has many attractive attributes, including its precision, small number of assumptions, muted sensitivities, and auditability. However, the model is not necessarily appropriate in all circumstances. The underlying assumption of lognormality may not be appropriate for some companies, and may limit the usefulness of the backsolve technique for determining implied total equity values. In our view, the model is best used in conjunction with the PWERM. Finally, as with all fair value measurement models, valuation specialists should carefully evaluate the degree to which the results of the model cohere with the market participant perspective.

37

Consequences of Calcified Cap Charts: A Few Thoughts on Startup Equity-Based Compensation

Sujan Rajbhandary, CFA
Originally Published on February 27, 2015

"You only find out who is swimming naked when the tide goes out."

– Warren Buffett

In a prior blog post, we noted a plethora of pricing indications observed around Box, Inc.'s (NYSE: BOX) initial public offering and asked the question, "Which price is right?" The prices (and implied valuations) that a business venture can obtain in future funding rounds, and in the public markets, are important considerations from the perspective of VCs and other investors. Unlike most mature public companies, however, startups have a predilection for complex capital structures, which introduces a degree of opacity that makes simple inference from headline numbers (however correct, however precise) difficult. A future funding round or exit event can result in varying outcomes for the multiple classes of securities with dissimilar rights and protections. This blog post will focus on the impact of (relatively steep) pre-public pricing on equity granted as employee compensation, usually the junior-most security in a startup capital stack.

Lay of the Land

Startup unicorns (pre-public companies with implied valuations exceeding $1 billion) are currently receiving plenty of press.[1] While a broad swath of investors (even mutual funds traditionally focused on public companies) appear to be in a race to grab a piece of the unicorn pie, some founders are equally willing to reciprocate with a penchant for status rounds that "gives [them] credibility and the ability to hire some very important people." Not all market participants, however, are sanguine about the dizzying escalation in the implied valuations for some of the pre-public companies. In addition to noting that investors rarely, if ever, subject a startup funding round to the same level of scrutiny faced by companies preparing to go public, venture capitalist Bill Gurley was quoted a few weeks ago opining on the potentially pernicious effect of a downturn in the pricing of pre-public companies:

> *"[At very high valuations] the cap chart begins to calcify a bit, which eventually can be problematic. Hiring new employees, particularly senior management, becomes tough because they worry about getting stuck beneath a huge liquidation preference stack. Some of these deals have so many [anti-dilution terms] that the cap table becomes almost concrete. If the valuation goes down significantly, it will sink them."*

> *"I think you're going to see a lot of failure in 2015. If you're a public company worth $3 billion and your stock trades down to $1 billion, you can survive it because you can still issue options to hire new employees, etc. If it happens when you're private, though, it becomes immediately harder to hire or to get incremental investment."* [2]

Stick Figure Cap Table

Mr. Gurley's concern can perhaps be illustrated using a relatively threadbare fictitious capital structure. A couple of (independently wealthy) entrepreneurs found Company A at Date 0, and proceed to introduce a disruptive technology and begin to achieve some market traction. At a subsequent Date 1, Company A raises $19 million in equity by issuing 950,000 Series X Preferred at $20 per share. Venture capital investors and the founders participate in the Series X round. Concurrently, Company A also reserves 50,000 Common shares for the purpose of granting equity compensation to its employees (restricted shares and/or stock options). The Series X Preferred shares have the following rights and downside protections:

- **Liquidation preferences** equal to 1.15x invested capital ($21.85 million). The liquidation preference would not be available in the case of an IPO exit.

- **Conversion rights** to exchange the Series X Preferred for Common shares at $20 per share.

- **Full ratchet protection** to convert Series X Preferred to Common at a lower price per share immediately prior to a future funding event if there is a down round (or, an IPO at a price lower than $20 per share).

Based on the fully diluted count (1,000,000 shares), the implied post money enterprise value of Company A is $20 million at Date 1.

Consider two exit scenarios for Company A at a subsequent Date 2.

- An IPO to sell (new) 150,000 Common shares at $15 per share. Pursuant to the ratchet, Series X Preferred shares would convert to 1,266,667 Common shares immediately preceding the IPO. Based on the fully diluted count (1,466,667 Common shares), the implied enterprise value is $22 million.

- A sale of Company A for $22 million. Pursuant to the liquidation preference, Series X Preferred holders receive $21.85 million, and Common shareholders (employees) receive the balance of the proceeds from the sale ($150,000).

On a fully diluted basis, Common shares granted as equity compensation represent 5.0% of the total capital at Date 1 (nominal value of $20 per share – see discussion in a subsequent section). Under the IPO scenario, the employees' stake in the Company is reduced to 3.4% (50,000 of 1,466,667 shares) at Date 2. If instead a sale of the Company were to occur, employees could only lay claim to a mere 0.7% of the total proceeds ($150,000 of $22 million).

Note that even as this example assumes a modest increase in the implied (post money) enterprise value between Dates 1 and 2, the value of the securities

Figure 37.1

Event	Date 0 Founding	Date 1 Funding	Date 2 - Alt 1 Exit - IPO	Date 2 - Alt 2 Exit - Strategic
Transaction Price	na	$20/share Ser X Preferred	$15/share Common	$22 million (Company sale)
Securities Issued	(nominal) Common Shares	950,000 Series X Preferred 50,000 Common (equiv.)	150,000 Common	None
Funds Raised	na	$19 million	$2.25 million	$22 million
Cumulative Share Count	(nominal) Common Shares	950,000 Series X Preferred 50,000 Common (comp)	1,266,667 Common (Ser X) 50,000 Common (comp) 150,000 Common (new)	950,000 Series X Preferred 50,000 Common
Total Share Count (Fully Diluted)	(nominal)	1,000,000	1,466,667	nm
Post-Money Valuation	na	$20 million	$22 million	$22 million

granted as employee compensation declines significantly. An exit that has to be consummated at a lower implied valuation would further erode any value (theoretically) realizable by the employees.

Real Consequences

In practice, the value of equity securities granted as employee compensation (common shares) should be different from the fully diluted economics presented in the preceding fictitious example. For example, according to its prospectus, factors that BOX reportedly considered in valuing common shares prior to its IPO included (partial list):

Figure 37.2: Stick Figure Cap Table

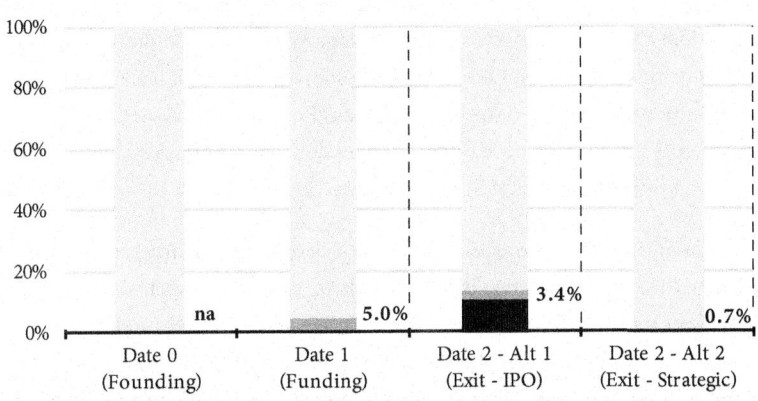

	Date 0	Date 1	Date 2 - Alt 1	Date 2 - Alt 2
Employee Ownership	0.0%	5.0%	3.4%	0.7%
Employee Comp Value	na	$1,000,000	$750,000	$150,000
	na	$20/share	$15/share	$3/share

- Contemporaneous valuations performed by unrelated third-party specialists.

- The prices, rights, preferences, and privileges of [BOX] redeemable convertible preferred stock relative to those of [BOX] common stock.

- Lack of marketability of [BOX] common stock.

- Likelihood of achieving a liquidity event, such as an initial public offering or a merger or acquisition of [BOX] given prevailing market conditions.

- Illiquidity of stock-based awards involving securities in a private company.

- Recent private stock sales transactions.

Valuation specialists can employ the probability-weighted expected return method (PWERM) to evaluate potential proceeds from, and the likelihood of, several exit scenarios for a company including dissolution/liquidation, average performance, or spectacular results. Total proceeds available in each scenario would then be allocated to the various classes of equity based on their rights and protections. Alternately, if visibility around the future exit prospects for the company is low, practitioners can use the option pricing method (OPM) to explicitly model the rights of each equity class, and make generalized assumptions about the future trajectory of the company to deduce values for the various securities. Under the OPM rubric, in some situations a backsolve procedure to infer values of certain securities based on recent transaction prices of other equity classes may be feasible. On occasion, valuation specialists also use a Hybrid of PWERM and OPM as relevant/necessary.

Differential rights and protections, and the lack of marketability typically associated with common shares, usually result in valuation conclusions that are lower than the fully diluted indications implied by preferred funding rounds. In theory, the lower value conclusion at the date of grant should dampen the subsequent reduction in value of the common shares if a down round were to occur in the future. Nevertheless, two tax issues around equity compensation can have meaningful, negative impact on employee compensation in the event of a down round.[3]

- **Section 409A of the Internal Revenue Code (IRC)** mandates that for stock options (or other derivative instruments) granted as equity compensation, the strike price should not be less than the grant date fair market value of the underlying stock. IRS Revenue Ruling 59-60 defines fair market value as "the price at which the property would change hands between a willing buyer and a willing seller when the former is not under any compulsion to buy and the latter is not under any compulsion to sell, both parties having reasonable knowledge of relevant facts." Specifically as it relates to startups, Section 409A states that a valuation will be presumed reasonable if "made reasonably and in good faith and evidenced by a written report that takes into account the relevant factors prescribed for valuations generally under these regulations." Pursuant to these guidelines and general practice, prices from recent transactions usually carry significant weight in a valuation specialist's determination of fair market value of the underlying stock. Accordingly, down rounds effectively raise the hurdle for options granted at prior periods before they can be valuable to the employees.

- **An IRC Section 83(b) election** allows an employee receiving equity compensation in the form of restricted stock to pay income taxes based on the fair market value of the award at the grant date. Increases in stock prices subsequent to the grant date are taxed at capital gains rates. If such an election is not made, employees are liable for income taxes based on the fair market value of the award as the restricted shares vest. It is easy to see how employees receiving restricted shares and making a Section 83(b) election can benefit if the price of the stock rises between the grant and vesting dates (provided other conditions for vesting are satisfied). In the case of a down round, or if an IPO (and subsequent trading) occurs at prices lower than at prior grant dates, however, the employees will have already paid (certain) taxes based on a higher value for a security that is worth less (and vesting may yet be uncertain).

Some Observations

Whatever the prospects of the current crop of highly valued late-stage pre-IPO companies as a group, it is not inconceivable that some of the individual companies will experience difficulty in growing into their valuations. Fab.com is an oft-cited reminder of how things can go wrong. The company raised $150 million at an implied enterprise value of $1 billion in June 2013. Cumulative funding obtained by the company totaled approximately $330 million. Within four months of the last funding round, however, the company changed tack and let go of hundreds of its employees. While the founder has reportedly pivoted into a newer venture, the company could be sold for a total consideration (including cash and stock) of $15 million.

BOX's story around and since the IPO, admittedly a lot less dramatic than Fab, also provides a couple of interesting data points from a valuation perspective. Prior to the IPO, BOX prepared several valuations of its common stock over a period of approximately two years.

A few observations:

- On two of the valuation dates (October 11, 2013 and July 7, 2014), BOX raised external funding rounds near-concurrently. The

Figure 37.3

	Valuation Dates			
	Feb 6, 2013	Jun 14, 2013	Oct 11, 2013	Jan 13, 2014
Concurrent Funding Round	None	None	Series E-1 $18.00/share	None
Valuation Approaches & Method(s) to Allocate Equity Value	Market Comparable cos Comparable M&A Income OPM	Market Comparable cos Comparable M&A Income OPM	OPM Backsolve Subsequent revision based on IPO prospects	Hybrid IPO (55% weight) Market comps Prior sale (Series E-1) Non-IPO (45%) OPM
Other Valuation Considerations	Secondary sale 496,340 shares $12.00 per share No Weight	None	None	Secondary sale 32,626 shares $24.25 per share 10% Weight
Discount Rate	45%	43%	na	35%
OPM Volatility	na	na	50%	45%
Nonmarketability Disc.	23%	27%	15%	10% - 20%
Value Conclusion Common per Share	$4.63	$6.13	$10.10	$14.06

Source: Company filings, Mercer Capital analysis

conclusion of value for the common shares represents a clear discount from the price commanded by the more senior shares at each of these valuation dates.

- The conclusion of value for common shares at the March 28, 2014 valuation date was $17.85, higher than the eventual IPO price of $14.00 per share on January 22, 2015.

Figure 37.3 (continued)

	Valuation Dates			
	Mar 28, 2014	Jul 7, 2014	Sep 15, 2014	Dec 3, 2014
Concurrent Funding Round	None	Series F $20.00/share	None	None
Valuation Approaches & Method(s) to Allocate Equity Value	Hybrid IPO (90%) Market comps Non-IPO (10%) OPM	Hybrid IPO (75%) Market comps Non-IPO (25%) OPM	Hybrid IPO (75%) Market comps Non-IPO (25%) OPM	Hybrid IPO (90%) Market comps Non-IPO (10%) OPM
Other Valuation Considerations	Secondary sale 32,626 shares $24.25 per share 10% Weight	Secondary sale 71,126 shares $29.67 per share 10% Weight	Secondary sale 71,126 shares $29.67 per share 10% Weight	None
Discount Rate	25%	25%	25%	25%
OPM Volatility	45%	45%	40%	40%
Nonmarketability Disc.	5% - 20%	5% - 20%	8% - 20%	5% - 20%
Value Conclusion Common per Share	$17.85	$12.79	$13.05	$14.05

Source: Company filings, Mercer Capital analysis

- On four valuation dates, pricing indications from secondary sales of common shares were accorded modest weights. Close to the January 13, 2014 and March 28, 2014 valuations dates, 32,626 common shares transacted at an average price of $24.25 per share. Near the July 7, 2014 and September 15, 2014 valuations dates, 71,126 common shares transacted at an average price of $29.67 per share.

Chart 37.1: BOX Common Stock Prices

Feb 6, 2013 to Feb 23, 2015

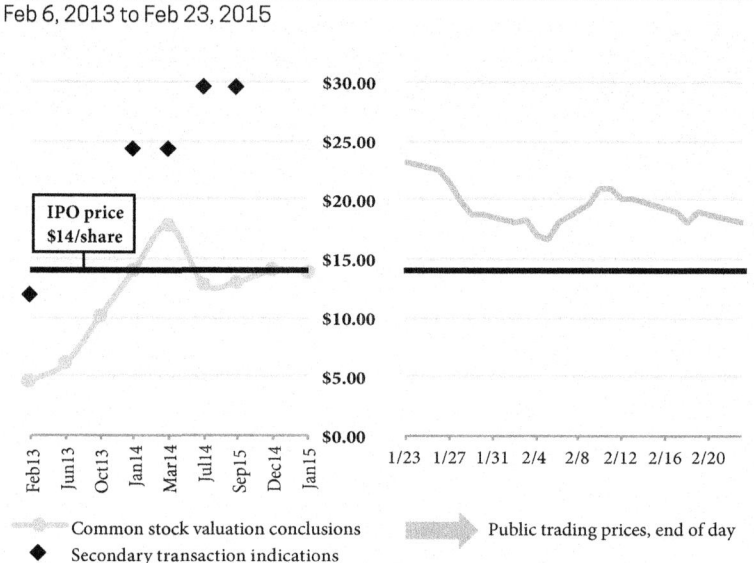

Source: *Company filings, Mercer Capital analysis*

- Trading closed at $23.23 on January 23, 2014, the first day after the IPO, but the price has since generally trended lower and closed at $18.21 on February 23, 2015. Notably, during the first calendar month of public trading, BOX's daily closing price has remained below the secondary pricing indications of $24.25 and $29.67 reported by the company between January and September 2014.

An Eye to the Future

While a couple of cherry-picked observations do not a trend make, if something that has gone up does indeed come down for some of the individual pre-public companies, investors, founders and other stakeholders will surely feel the pain. As we discuss in this blog post, the impact of a pricing downturn will likely be asymmetrical across the capital structure owing to the differential rights and protections accorded to the various securities. In particular, in the case of equity-based compensation granted to employees, unwarranted optimism regarding the prospects of the employer company coupled with certain tax rules and choices may result in real, negative economic impact. Unfortunately, only hindsight may be a good enough judge of whether decisions being made today, by employees and investors alike, will turn out to be prudent.

End Notes

[1]   For more information, see Griffith, Erin and Dan Primack. "The Age of Unicorns." Fortune. January 22, 2015. http://fortune.com/2015/01/22/the-age-of-unicorns/

[2]   Primack, Dan. "Top VC: A lot of tech startup failure coming in 2015" Fortune. January 22, 2015. http://fortune.com/2015/01/22/vc-tech-startup-failure-2015/

[3]   We are not tax experts. Those interested in specific guidance for tax or legal matters should seek competent professional advice.

38

Market Participant Perspectives: An Inside Look at the YouTube Seed Round

Travis W. Harms, CFA, CPA/ABV
Originally Published on May 9, 2014

A timely issue of Fortune's daily Term Sheet included a link to a copy of documents relating to YouTube's 2005 seed round fundraising. The documents, attached to a 2010 court filing, include the presentation made by YouTube's founders to potential investors and an internal investment memorandum from Roelof Botha, partner at Sequoia Capital, outlining the rationale for an investment in the Company.[1]

The documents provide a fascinating peek behind the curtain, demonstrating what actual market participants care about (and don't care about) when evaluating early-stage companies. For valuation specialists preparing fair value measurements of early-stage companies, the documents are great reminders of the key elements of start-up valuation. In this post, we highlight a few of the primary themes.

- **Comparison to Observed Trends**. While YouTube's file sharing technology was clearly a critical factor in the Company's success (and valuation), the lead VC supporting the investment focused on the broader trends in user-generated content when evaluating YouTube's potential. Although a novel technology, YouTube's video-sharing service was a natural evolution of the broader user-generated content sharing trend which was manifest in the success and popularity of blogs (sharing user-generated written communication) and sites like Flickr (sharing user-generated still photos).

- **Importance of Enabling Technologies**. According to the investment memorandum, two enabling technologies were paving the way for YouTube's growth at that particular time: the proliferation of relatively inexpensive digital video recording devices and the spread of broadband internet access. YouTube's file-sharing technology was not an isolated engineering feat, but represented a timely "fit" with other technological changes in the broader market.

- **A Clearly Identified Problem**. Why did the world need YouTube? Video files were bulky and in a variety of file formats (and therefore difficult to share). In addition, by serving as a reputable central "clearinghouse" for user-generated content, YouTube would help meet the need for community among individuals with common interests.

- **Focus on Human Capital**. The experience and track record of YouTube's three co-founders was prominent in the investment memorandum. It is clear that Sequoia was investing in people as much as in technology. Even so, the investment memorandum acknowledged the need for additional management resources and leadership to support the Company's growth and development.

- **A Clear-Eyed View of the Competition**. Given the observed trends, growth and availability of enabling technologies and the defined problem, YouTube was not the only potential solution hitting the market. The investment memorandum carefully evaluated, classified, and compared competing product offerings.

- **Revenue Thesis**. Despite being at the pre-revenue stage, alternatives for generating revenue (primarily through advertising) were identified. Revenue (and profitability) was the ultimate objective, and even though precise forecasts were not feasible, identification of the means by which YouTube would earn revenue was not deferred to a later date.

- **Personal Experience**. Mr. Botha reported being drawn to the investment opportunity, in part, because he had used the site himself.

Obviously, not all innovative products lend themselves to sampling, but the threshold question of "Why YouTube?" was, at least initially, answered through personal experience of the company's service offering.

Somewhat disconcerting for valuation specialists is what the investment memorandum did not include: financial forecasts, discount rates, probability factors, or option-pricing model equity allocation analyses. The absence of these valuation tools does not mean they should be dropped from the specialist's toolbox – they are indispensable for providing an audit trail – but does suggest that the tools need to be used with consistent reference to the "qualitative" factors discussed in the YouTube investment memorandum. The credibility of the valuation analysis will depend upon it.

End Note

[1]   The documents are available at http://hadley.sharedby.co/share/n6ps9w

39

Rest and Vest

Lucas Parris, CFA, ASA-BV/IA
Originally Published on September 3, 2014

The HBO sitcom *Silicon Valley* follows the story of six young, tech-savvy, would-be entrepreneurs who found a start-up company. The show depicts the ups and downs of the characters and their company, Pied Piper, against a backdrop of both real-world and semi-fictional companies, tech celebrities, venture capitalists, and other cultural phenomena of Silicon Valley.

Several characters have day jobs at a large, successful technology company called Hooli. Early in the series, a character nicknamed Big Head is offered a raise and promotion by the boss of Hooli. Big Head accepts the offer, but is shocked and confused when he is subsequently told that he won't be assigned to any new projects. But he's not being fired, either. As Big Head wanders the halls of Hooli trying to make sense of things, he stumbles upon a group of guys hanging out on the roof of the building who are similarly "unassigned" at Hooli. He's invited into their group, where the following exchange takes place.

> *Unassigned Hooli Employee: "We all got acquired by Hooli, and when we didn't work out, none of us got reassigned...."*
>
> *Big Head: "Why are you guys still coming in?"*
>
> *Unassigned Hooli Employee: "Rest and vest."*

Big Head: "Oh... Cause in order to fully vest your options, you've got to wait until your contracts are up. I get it."

Another Unassigned Hooli Employee: "You catch on slow. You'll fit right in here."

The "rest and vest" scenario is a real thing, though it is debatable how accurately it is presented in the show. There are also obvious differences between the perception of the value of options received by an employee and the financial reporting requirements of the issuing company. In the world of financial reporting, vesting conditions can affect both the grant-date fair value of a stock award as well as the period over which the compensation cost is recognized by the issuing company. "Rest and vest" referenced in Silicon Valley reflects the fulfillment of a service condition in the parlance of ASC 718: Compensation – Stock Compensation. Service conditions are most often time-based. However, many stock-based awards could also include additional conditions that must be met in order for the award to vest. Some of these conditions affect the grant-date fair value of the award and some do not. Figure 39.1 summarizes the three types of vesting conditions as described in ASC 718.

The measurement objective of ASC 718 is to determine the grant-date fair value of the compensation, assuming the employee fulfills the award's vesting

Figure 39.1

Vesting Condition	Considered in Grant-Date Fair Value?	Example
Service Condition	No	Vesting based on an employee rendering service for specified length of time or accelerated conditions for death, disability, termination clauses
Market Condition	Yes	Vesting based on issuer's share price performance or movement relative to an index of peer companies
Performance Condition	No	Vesting based on company profitability targets or company activities/events (such as IPO or change in control)

conditions and retains the award. That compensation amount is then recognized over the requisite service period. The requisite service period may be explicitly or implicitly stated in the terms of the award, such as a simple award that vests in graded increments over a number of years of continuous service. In other cases, the requisite service period may need to be derived, such as in the case of an award subject to market condition vesting (i.e., award becomes exercisable only if the issuer's stock rises by 25% at any time during a three year period).

All else equal, an award with a market condition "hurdle" will have a lower grant-date fair value than one that does not. Then, if the award contains service and/or performance conditions, those conditions would be incorporated into the company's estimate of what percentage of the award will ultimately vest. For instance, management of the company would need to assess the likelihood that performance conditions (such as an IPO or change in control) will be achieved. These estimates then affect the amount of compensation cost recognized in each reporting period.

Estimating the fair value of stock-based compensation and accounting for it properly can be complex. Maybe it's more appealing to envy the "unassigned" employee just biding his time as he rests and vests. Then again, why doesn't the company just terminate the "unassigned" employee for cause and cancel his options since the venture didn't work out? I guess that's why they call it a television show.

Equity-Based Compensation: Are Non-GAAP Earnings Misleading?

Travis W. Harms, CFA, CPA/ABV
Originally Published on August 28, 2015

During the 1990s debate over the status of stock options as a corporate expense, the big technology companies argued passionately that, since stock option grants to employees don't ding the corporate checkbook, they should not be recognized as an expense. Despite winning the initial battle (SFAS 123), the tech companies ultimately lost the war (SFAS 123R).

As noted in an article by Tim Shufelt, many big-name tech companies include, as a non-GAAP measure of financial performance, earnings exclusive of the despised stock-based compensation charge.[1] Not surprisingly, earnings without the options-related charges are considerably more robust for highfliers like Amazon and Netflix. For example, in its investor slide deck for the Q3, 2013 earnings call, Amazon touts a non-GAAP earnings measure called "Consolidated Segment Operating Income" or "CSOI". The principal reconciling item between CSOI and GAAP Operating Income is stock-based compensation. For the twelve months ended September 30, 2012, CSOI was $1.795 billion, or 2.8x GAAP operating income of $640 million.

Amazon's 10-Q for the quarter ended September 30, 2013 offers the following justification for excluding stock-based compensation from measures like CSOI:

"Operating expenses with and without stock-based compensation is provided to show the impact of stock-based compensation, which is

non-cash and excluded from our internal operating plans and measurement of financial performance (although we consider the dilutive impact to our shareholders when awarding stock-based compensation and value such awards accordingly). In addition, unlike other centrally-incurred operating costs, stock-based compensation is not allocated to segment results and therefore excluding it from operating expense is consistent with our segment presentation in our footnotes to the consolidated financial statements."

The 10-Q does acknowledge the drawbacks of excluding stock-based compensation from earnings, effectively summarizing the prevailing rationale for including such compensation as an expense:

"Operating expenses without stock-based compensation has limitations since it does not include all expenses primarily related to our workforce. More specifically, if we did not pay out a portion of our compensation in the form of stock-based compensation, our cash salary expenses included in the 'Fulfillment,' 'Marketing,' 'Technology and content,' and 'General and administrative' line items would be higher.

From a valuation standpoint, it is noteworthy that the rationale for the adjustment is supported, not by the expectation that such grants are unusual or non-recurring, but rather by the fact that the grants do not immediately consume corporate cash. However, as acknowledged by Amazon, cash is preserved only at the expense of shareholder dilution, a very real albeit "soft" cost. Regardless of the ongoing debate about how best to measure earnings, stock-based compensation is a tool used by companies of all sizes and in all industries. In order to deliver the most reliable information to investors, companies need to carefully evaluate the value of such compensation packages when granted.

End Note

[1]   Shufelt, Tim. "Double Standard: the tech sector's love affair with adjusted earnings." The Globe and Mail. November 22, 2013. http://www.theglobeandmail.com/globe-investor/investment-ideas/tech-sectors-double-standard/article15555227/

About the Authors

Travis W. Harms, CFA, CPA/ABV

901.685.2120 | harmst@mercercapital.com

Travis leads Mercer Capital's Financial Reporting Valuation Group. Travis's practice focuses on providing public and private clients with fair value opinions and related assistance pertaining to goodwill and other intangible assets, stock-based compensation, and illiquid financial assets.

Travis also leads Mercer Capital's Private Equity industry team and publishes a quarterly newsletter, *Portfolio Valuation: Private Equity Marks & Trends*.

Travis is a frequent speaker on fair value accounting topics to audiences of financial executives, auditors, and valuation specialists at professional conferences and other events across the U.S.

Lucas Parris, CFA, ASA-BV/IA

901.322.9784 | parrisl@mercercapital.com

Lucas Parris is a senior member of Mercer Capital's Financial Reporting Valuation Group, providing public and private clients with fair value opinions and related assistance pertaining to goodwill and other intangible assets, stock-based compensation, and illiquid financial assets.

Lucas also has valuation experience in engagements related to corporate planning and reorganizations, litigation support, employee stock ownership plans, and estate and gift tax planning and compliance matters. Valuation opinions prepared by Lucas have been accepted by each of the four largest U.S. audit firms and various regulatory bodies, including the IRS.

Sujan Rajbhandary, CFA

901.322.9749 | sujanr@mercercapital.com

Sujan Rajbhandary, vice president, is a senior member of Mercer Capital's Financial Reporting Valuation Group, which provides fair value opinions and related advisory services to public companies, private companies, and alternative investment vehicles.

Sujan has valued financial assets and liabilities for litigation support, tax compliance, ESOP compliance, and shareholder transactions.

Samantha L. Albert

901.322.9702 | alberts@mercercapital.com

Samantha Albert is a senior financial analyst with Mercer Capital. Samantha is experienced in the valuation of companies across a variety of industries, and has considerable experience working with animal health practices and related enterprises. As a member of the Financial Reporting Valuation Group, she provides valuation analyses related to intangible assets, contractual agreements, and complex capital structures. Samantha also works regularly on complex valuation assignments related to litigated matters.

In addition, Samantha assists with the production of *The National Economic Review*. The product, one of many available from Mercer Capital's extensive research services portfolio, provides a consensus quarterly review of the national economy to hundreds of business valuation professionals across the country.

Karolina Calhoun, CPA/ABV

901.322.9761 | calhounk@mercercapital.com

Karolina Calhoun is a senior financial analyst with Mercer Capital. As a member of the Financial Reporting Valuation Group, Karolina provides valuation analyses related to intangible assets, contractual agreements, and complex capital structures.

She also provides valuation services for purposes such as estate and gift tax planning, employee stock ownership plans, and corporate planning.

Mary Grace McQuiston

901.322.9720 | mcquistonm@mercercapital.com

Mary Grace McQuiston is a senior financial analyst with Mercer Capital. Mary Grace is experienced in the valuation of financial institutions, particularly depository institutions, business development companies, and related enterprises. As a member of Mercer Capital's Financial Institutions Group, she prepares valuation analyses related to transactions, fairness opinions, equity compensation arrangements, shareholder agreements, and other circumstances.

Taryn E. Burgess

901.322.9757 | burgesst@mercercapital.com

Taryn Burgess is a financial analyst with Mercer Capital. Taryn is involved in the valuation of public and private companies, as well as financial institutions, employee stock ownership plans, estate and gift tax planning, and other corporate entities.

Mercer Capital's
Financial Reporting Blog

The Financial Reporting Blog is a weekly update on financial reporting topics curated by Mercer Capital's Financial Reporting Valuation professionals.

Topics Covered:

- Bankruptcy and Restructuring Advisory
- Equity-Based Compensation Valuation
- Fair Value
- Impairment Testing
- Markets
- Portfolio Valuation
- Purchase Price Allocation
- Tax

Subscribe at mercercapital.com/financialreportingblog

Mercer Capital's Financial Reporting Valuation Services

In an environment of increasingly complex fair value reporting standards and burgeoning regulatory scrutiny, Mercer Capital helps clients resolve financial reporting valuation issues successfully.

We have the capability to serve the full range of fair value valuation needs, providing valuation opinions that satisfy the scrutiny of auditors, the SEC, and other regulatory bodies.

We also have broad experience with fair value issues related to public and private companies, financial institutions, private equity firms, start-up enterprises, and other closely held businesses. National audit firms consistently refer financial reporting valuation assignments to Mercer Capital.

Financial Reporting Valuation Services:

- Bankruptcy and Restructuring Advisory
- Equity-Based Compensation Valuation
- 280G Golden Parachute Valuation
- Impairment Testing
- Portfolio Valuation Services
- Purchase Price Allocation

Contact a Mercer Capital professional to discuss your needs in confidence.
901.685.2120 | www.mercercapital.com

CPSIA information can be obtained
at www.ICGtesting.com
Printed in the USA
LVOW13s1924081116

512183LV00001B/1/P